S0-CFZ-074

PUNISHMENT SEASON

HUMAN RIGHTS IN CHINA
AFTER MARTIAL LAW

An Asia Watch Report

March 1990

Punishment Season: Human Rights in China after Martial Law
© 1990 by the Asia Watch Committee.
All rights reserved.
Printed in the United States of America.
ISBN 0-929-629-51-9
Cost: $10.00 per copy

THE ASIA WATCH COMMITTEE

The Asia Watch Committee was established in 1985 to monitor and promote observance of internationally recognized human rights in Asia. The Executive Director is Sidney Jones, the Chairman is Jack Greenberg and the Vice Chairmen are Matthew Nimetz and Nadine Strossen.

HUMAN RIGHTS WATCH

Human Rights Watch comprises Africa Watch, Americas Watch, Asia Watch, Helsinki Watch and Middle East Watch. The Chairman is Robert L. Bernstein, the Vice Chairman is Adrian DeWind. The Executive Director is Aryeh Neier and Kenneth Roth is Deputy Director. For further information, including a full publications list with subscription forms or an annual report, please write to:

Human Rights Watch
485 Fifth Avenue
New York, NY 10017
(212) 972-8400
Fax (212) 972-0905

Human Rights Watch
1522 K Street N.W., Suite 910
Washington, DC 20005
(202) 371-6592
Fax (202) 371-0124

Att. Publications Coordinator

CONTENTS

ACKNOWLEDGEMENTS

This report was written by Robin Munro, Asia Watch's staff specialist on China. A long-time observer of China's democracy movement, Robin Munro was in Beijing during the weeks leading up to the June 3-4 military attack on the students and workers. He was in Tiananmen Square throughout the night of the assault and remained in Beijing until June 20.

The chapter entitled "The Bush Administration's Response" was written by Holly Burkhalter, the Washington Director of Human Rights Watch. In addition, Asia Watch gratefully acknowledges the assistance of Marianne Spiegel in helping to compile the information on arrests and executions that appears in the Appendix to this report. J. Lewis also gave valuable assistance.

* The title of this report — "Punishment Season" — derives from a Chinese saying that was often used by the students in Tiananmen Square: **"qiu hou suan zhang"** (the Chinese characters on the front cover). Literally, the saying means "to settle accounts after the autumn harvest," but its real meaning is: **"to take vengeance when the time is ripe."** The students always knew that the government, sooner or later, would do this. The government, right up until June 4, indignantly denied it...

INTRODUCTION

The recent lifting of martial law in Beijing (though not, it should be remembered, in Lhasa) has little significance if viewed as anything other than a public relations exercise — and as one designed largely for international, and especially US Congressional, consumption. Having successfully bludgeoned the population of Beijing into temporary submission, and having installed a fearsome network of vigilante, police and paramilitary forces throughout the Chinese capital in order to maintain the repression, the authorities can now easily afford to dispense with the formal institution of martial law and to return the People's Liberation Army to barracks. Western diplomats in Beijing report that the troops have largely been relocated in the suburbs of the capital, rather than having been returned to their original provinces. They also note that tens of thousands of them still remain in the capital, having merely exchanged their PLA uniforms for those of the semi-civilian, paramilitary People's Armed Police.[*]

Other world leaders were not impressed by this move, but President Bush, anxious to be able to show some kind of result from his excessively conciliatory policy towards Beijing since last June, uncritically endorsed it as being "a good sign" and "a very sound step."[**]

The US administration's expectation that tangible improvements in the human rights situation in China are just around the corner, and its view that the best way to ensure these is to minimize the degree of external diplomatic criticism and pressure that is brought to bear upon the present Chinese regime,

---

[*]   Washington Post, January 11, 1990. According to Ming Bao (January 12), 40,000 troops have been re-equipped as People's Armed Police.

[**]   New York Times, January 12, 1990.

1

are entirely unsupported by the facts. Although less visible than before, the repression — the "big chill" — nonetheless continues to develop apace, and in certain respects has substantially deepened. On November 29, 1989 the *New China News Agency* quoted a senior official of the Supreme People's Procuratorate, Zhang Siqing, as saying that China's prosecutors would give high priority this year to cracking down on "anti-government rioters and other major criminals." In 1990, prosecutors would continue "to comb out and suppress anti-government rioters and other criminals, including beaters, smashers, looters, burners and killers" (the official codewords for last year's pro-democracy demonstrators). This sentiment was reiterated as recently as January 8, 1990 by the President of the Supreme People's Court, Ren Jianxin: "Priority should also be given to cracking down on criminals harmful to social stability and dealing with the criminal cases arising from last year's unrest and riots."

On December 3, 1989 the *Washington Post*, citing Chinese sources, reported:

> The authorities recently launched a new wave of investigations aimed at tracking down and prosecuting participants in the student-led democracy movement. The targets of the unannounced dragnet include student 'anti-government rioters' and Communist Party 'scum' who supported the movement last spring. In a recent, unpublicized speech, Beijing's hardline party chief, Li Ximing, expressed his dissatisfaction with the slowness of the hunt...

On China's campuses, which served as the main incubators of last year's pro-democracy movement, the atmosphere is grim. According to the Hong Kong newspaper *Ming Bao* of December 26, 1989:

> The Chinese People's Political Consultative Conference has

---

*   Cited in <u>South China Morning Post</u>, November 30, 1989.

**   <u>Foreign Broadcast Information Service</u> (hereinafter cited as <u>FBIS</u>), January 11, 1990.

2

suggested that severe punishment be meted out to those young and middle-aged university teachers who still refuse to repent and mend their ways and who are suspected of 'acting as evil backstage manipulators.'

The recent announcement by the Chinese authorities (again, apparently, timed to coincide with the re-opening of Congress) that 573 detainees have now been released** is in essence a publicity stunt. If true, the move is of course to be welcomed. But the fact is that anywhere between 10,000 and 30,000 people, according to independent Western estimates, remain behind bars in China on account of their pro-democracy activities last summer. The great majority of these are ordinary workers who (unlike many of the detained students and intellectuals) have no contact whatever with the outside world, and their fate is thus impossible to monitor at present. The Chinese government has shown an iron fist to the extensive independent workers' movement that emerged throughout China last May, and there is no indication that it will slacken, even slightly, this campaign of repression at the grassroots level.

As a minimum step, the Chinese authorities should now publish a full list of names of the 573 persons recently reported to have been released. Furthermore, Asia Watch invites the Chinese government to allow our organization to send a formal mission to Beijing in order to verify the releases and to ascertain the numbers of those still detained and their conditions of detention.

While presenting internationally the lifting of martial law as being a proof of the crackdown's end, the authorities have taken pains to ensure that the Chinese people receive a different message. According to a *People's Daily* editorial of January 11:

> The lifting of martial law does not mean peace and tranquility across the land. International reactionary forces are bent on subjugating our country. A handful of stubborn bourgeois liberalists at home are not reconciled to their defeat. After our victory in curbing the turmoil and quelling the counter-

---

* In FBIS, December 26, 1989.

** New York Times, January 19, 1990. Significantly: "A public security official said those released had pleaded guilty and shown repentance." Note that no "innocent" people were released. In China, "lenience" is the reward of contrition, not of innocence.

revolutionary rebellion and the lifting of martial law, we must not lose our vigilance....We should deal a timely and forceful blow at the sabotage by hostile forces, and those who violate the law should be sternly dealt with according to law.*

Chinese sources report an official but undeclared policy of "outward relaxation, internal intensification" (*waisong neijin*) to be now operating as regards the crackdown in China. According to the US-based *Shijie Ribao* (World Journal, December 14, 1989), Premier Li Peng's recent statement to the editor of the West German *Die Welt* that "those who took part in marches, demonstrations or hunger strikes, and those who supported them...will all be dealt with leniently...and not punished at all," was later flatly contradicted in an internal directive issued to the provinces by the Office of the Communist Party Central Committee. Citing an unnamed official from the latter organ, *Shijie Ribao* revealed that this internal directive had ordered the localities, in dealing with pro-democracy activists, "to eradicate the evil once and for all, and to leave no vestiges of the plague"; Li Peng's comment to *Die Welt* was merely "directed to the outside world, for propaganda effect," said the official.

On the very day of the ostensible lifting of martial law in Beijing, at least four people were arrested in Tiananmen Square: two for attempting to lay a wreath in the Square, discreetly marked "in memory of those killed here by accident"; an elderly man for making sarcastic comments to policemen stationed at the Monument to the People's Heroes; and a middle-aged woman for daring to talk with a British television team.** All this is unrepentant Stalinism at its most wearily familiar, and it requires considerable naivete to see the recent cosmetic face-lift in Beijing as representing any substantive progress towards human rights.

In this report, Asia Watch seeks to underline the continuing serious nature of the repression in China by cataloguing in summary form the wide range of human rights abuses recently and currently being committed by the Chinese

---

* In FBIS, January 10, 1989.

** UPI, January 12, 1990; Shijie Ribao, January 13; South China Morning Post, January 12, in FBIS, same day.

authorities.[*]

*   Since the focus of this report is upon the recent and continuing human rights disaster in China, the report does not attempt to describe or summarize the wholesale and egregious violations of human rights committed by the Chinese authorities on June 3-4, 1989 and during the immediate aftermath.

1. ARRESTS AND EXECUTIONS

What are human rights? As understood by Western scholars, they are the innate rights of human beings, or the basic rights and freedoms enjoyed by a person as a human. They primarily consist of the rights to life, freedom, equality, property, self-defense and happiness, and the right to oppose persecution. These rights are innate, permanent, universal, and nontransferrable. They cannot be taken away....

In the context of Marxism, [however,] such an interpretation of human rights is unscientific, incorrect, contrived, biased and idealistically metaphysical... Human rights, like democracy and freedom, are concrete and class-oriented.

(*Guangming Daily*, November 17, 1989)

Since June 1989, the Chinese authorities have again been waging a war against the so-called "class enemy" — an elastic term that has been used to stigmatize countless different groups of people in China over the past forty years, but which currently denotes the students, workers and intellectuals who actively promoted or took part in last year's pro-democracy movement. Several hundred and perhaps as many as a thousand of these "counterrevolutionaries" were killed on the streets of Beijing by the Chinese army as it converged from all directions on Tiananmen Square on the night of June 3-4, and many thousands more have been hunted down and placed in incommunicado detention by the security forces since then. There have been at least 40 officially announced executions of pro-democracy demonstrators, and secret executions may also have occurred.[*] On November 4, 1989, *Reuters* quoted William Webster, head of the CIA, as saying that "probably thousands of people have been killed" since the crackdown first began.

In late June or early July, following the international outcry over the scale and severity of the crackdown, the authorities issued a confidential directive sharply curtailing the open reporting of arrests and executions in the Chinese media, in an effort to convey the impression that it had somehow diminished. But the arrests have continued, largely in secret, right through to the present, and reports of further executions having recently been carried out continue to appear in the provincial press, to which foreign observers have only restricted access.

According to Asia Watch's information, most of those detained have neither been charged nor brought to trial, and often their families have not even been informed as to their place of detention. Those people who have been brought to trial have been subjected to expedited and summary trial proceedings, under a system of justice which specifically rejects the principle of the presumption of innocence and in which (according to the Chinese authorities themselves) verdicts are usually decided upon before the trial even begins.

The majority of those brought to trial have been convicted on charges of "counterrevolution," a blatantly political category of criminal offense, and the sentences handed down in such cases have generally ranged from 10 years to life imprisonment. Others have simply been sentenced without any trial at all

---

[*] The Beijing correspondent of UPI reported on July 27, 1989 that more than 40 people had been secretly executed during the previous two weeks at Lugouqiao ('Marco Polo Bridge') in the suburbs of Beijing.

— usually to three year terms of "re-education through labor," a form of incarceration that is dispensed solely on the authority of the police.*

In most cases, the prison sentences handed down by the courts have been entirely disproportionate to the alleged crimes. In July 1989 for example, three men accused of throwing ink and paint-filled eggshells at Mao's portrait in Tiananmen Square in May were sentenced to prison terms ranging from 16 years to life. And on December 7, 1989, a worker in Changsha was sentenced to 13 years imprisonment for making pro-democracy speeches and engaging in independent labor union activity.**

Evidence that the Chinese authorities are specifically trying to conceal from the outside world the fact that the political trials still continue was provided by the *Washington Post* in December 1989:

> Two trial notices were posted outside the People's Intermediate Court in Beijing this week. One of the defendants was charged with 'counterrevolutionary sabotage'; the other with espionage and 'counterrevolutionary propaganda and agitation.' Court officials, reached by telephone, declined to comment on the two cases. One of them told a foreign reporter, 'You know that it's not permitted to ask questions like that.' When the reporter went to the court to photograph the posted trial notices, a court official ripped them down.***

---

* The chief "legal" basis for the practice of re-education through labor is the 1957 Decision of the State Council on the Question of Re-education Through Labor. Theoretically, a reform of 1979 embodied in the Supplementary Regulations on Re-education through Labor extended the power to impose this "administrative sanction" to bodies comprising authorities other than just the public security organs, in order to make its use less arbitrary. According to the Supplementary Regulations: "The people's governments at provincial, municipal and autonomous-regional levels, and those of large and medium-sized cities, shall establish Labor Re-Education Administrative Committees (LRACs), comprising responsible members of the departments of civil affairs, public security and labor deployment, in order to lead and adminster the work of re-education through labor....[These committees] shall examine and approve the cases of all persons requiring to undergo re-education." This reform remained a dead letter, however. According to the official Law Daily of February 10, 1988: "[Even now,] the work of examining and approving, and also of implementing, re-education through labor, is carried out solely by the public security authorities.....In practice, the majority of LRACs exist only in name. Some of them meet barely once a year, so the question of their being able to examine or approve cases is purely rhetorical."

** See Appendix: Zhang Jingsheng. .

*** Washington Post December 3, 1989.

9

The question of how many people have been arrested or detained since last June is — like the question of how many died in the military crackdown — extremely difficult to answer with any precision, and estimates vary greatly. By adding up various scattered figures put out by the Chinese authorities themselves, Western journalists last summer arrived at a total official arrest figure of at least 6000. In early December, *Beijing Youth News* disclosed that 2578 people had been arrested in connection with the pro-democracy movement in Beijing in the 24-day period following June 4, and that only 190 have since been released; moreover, this total referred only to so-called "ruffians" (or "thugs"), and it excludes all workers or students detained on non-violent and purely political charges.[*]

Other sources (cited by *UPI*), indicated that 6000 people had been arrested in Beijing alone by the end of July, and the *Washington Post* last October cited "sources with access to internal government documents" as putting the figure at more than 10,000 nationwide. Western diplomats interviewed in Beijing last November estimated that anywhere between 10,000 and 30,000 people had probably been arrested in China since the commencement of the crackdown. Citing "well-placed Communist Party sources," a recent article in the *Washington Post*[**] reported that more than 800 of those involved in last year's movement had already been tried and sentenced to prison terms in recent months, many for ten years on charges of divulging "state secrets" or disseminating "counterrevolutionary propaganda."

Even those injured by government troops on the night of June 3-4 reportedly continue to be persecuted by the authorities. According to an interview conducted in China in October 1989 by the *Star Tribune*:

> Wang was on a Beijing street, a curious bystander, when a soldier's bullet shattered his bones and marked him with a label he may never shed. As China continues its crackdown on the democracy movement that erupted in June, Wang and the other wounded are in great danger. The dead are beyond reach, the unmarked cannot be found, and so official wrath is

---

[*]   Agence France Presse, December 5, 1989; in FBIS, January 3, 1990.

[**]   January 17, 1990.

focussed on the injured. Investigators have endless questions. Why was he out in the streets? What slogans did he shout? What banner did he wave? Who else was around him?[*]

In addition, large numbers of students and workers are currently under active investigation by the authorities, on campuses and in the workplace, for their alleged activities during the events of last summer; to facilitate the purge, people are being cajoled by the authorities to inform upon one another. At one of Beijing's elite universities recently, a teacher interviewed by the *New York Times* "described a faculty meeting with the Party secretary, who complained that while some students had informed on others, no teachers had done so, behavior that set a bad example....We felt he had no sense of shame."[**] In at least two recent reported cases, students have committed suicide as a result of this intense official harassment and pressure.[***]

As for China's long-suffering intellectuals, who have been the target of repeated campaigns of persecution and intimidation since 1949, there are signs that their present plight may worsen still further. In December 1989, the Hong Kong journal *Bai Xing* reported that Wang Zhen, Vice-President of the PRC, had "proposed at a recent Party meeting that 4000 intellectuals in Beijing who stand opposed to the Party be sent into exile in Xinjiang," the north-west frontier province where China's vast Gulag lies, "so that they could be transformed there."[****]

Despite the crude severity of the government repression, China's pro-democracy movement has not been silenced completely. In a remarkable act of courage, 30 students from the Beijing Institute of Aeronautics on December 9,

---

[*]   Star Tribune (Minneapolis, Minn.), December 24, 1989.

[**]   New York Times, January 2, 1990. Reportedly: "The Party secretary was particularly outraged because he had received anonymous letters purporting to inform on him." Acccording to another, slightly earlier interview: "A professor, heaving a sigh, said: 'My students become cynical, suffer agonies, fall into despair, and are at a loss, and the school and students are changed beyond recognition.'" (FBIS, December 27, 1989.)

[***] Both were from Qinghua University, Beijing. According to the Hong Kong Standard of December 1, 1989, a postgraduate student named Tang Zujie, 23, jumped from a sixth-floor window on campus on October 1, China's National Day. An economics postgraduate named Guo Wei, 24, killed himself on November 2.

[****] Bai Xing, December 16, 1989; in FBIS, December 19.

1989 defied martial law by staging a protest march along central Chang'an Avenue and carrying banners saying "Freedom and Democracy" and "Why is China so poor?" They were promptly set upon and beaten by the police, and eight of them were taken into custody, though one later escaped. Onlookers, who had begged them to disperse, reportedly wept openly as the students were hauled away.* Revealing a striking — but characteristic — presumption of guilt, an Education Ministry spokesman later told *Reuters*: "These students' illegal assembly and speeches...break martial law. They are detained and awaiting their sentences."

(i) Arrests

The Chinese authorities' relentless hunt for scapegoats to blame for their drastic recent loss of popular support and legitimacy continues. Asia Watch has documented several dozen further arrests and trials of pro-democracy individuals that took place between October 1989 and January 1990, and has received reliable reports that many others (though names are not yet known) were arrested or tried over the same period. The following examples convey the general flavor of the continuing repression in China.

- Wang Juntao and Chen Ziming, two intellectuals who headed one of the Chinese authorities 'most wanted lists,' together with Chen's pregnant wife, Wang Zhihong, were arrested near Canton last October while reportedly trying to escape to Hong Kong. Three Hong Kong residents, Luo Haixing, Li Peicheng and Li Longqing, alleged to have been active in the underground rescue network, were also, between October and December, arrested in China in connection with the case. Wang Juntao and Chen Ziming are largely unknown in the West, but they were key figures in the 1989 pro-democracy movement. Indeed, both have played a major role in China's dissident movement ever since 1976, when they were arrested and jailed for helping to organize the popular mass demonstrations in Tiananmen Square against the regime of the "Gang of Four." During the "Democracy Wall" movement of 1978-80 (the forerunner of last year's movement), Wang Juntao

---

*   <u>Washington Post</u> December 14, 1989.

founded and edited an unofficial pro-democracy magazine called *Beijing Spring*. And in 1980 he stood as an independent candidate for the local Beijing legislature, in the first openly-contested elections ever to be held in the People's Republic.

Prior to last year's crackdown, Wang, 31, was a leading member of the Beijing Institute of Social and Economic Sciences and associate chief editor of the influential (and now banned) *Economic Studies Weekly*. Chen Ziming, 37-years-old and from Zhejiang Province, is also a leading veteran of the Democracy Wall movement. Until June 4, he was director of the Beijing Institute of Social and Economic Sciences, a pioneering private research organization and think-tank that worked closely with the Party's reform faction headed by Zhao Ziyang.

• On November 5, 1989, a man named Zhao Shujian was arrested in Henan Province for having allegedly spread "counterrevolutionary slogans." According to the *Henan Daily* of December 3:

> On 20 May this year, more than 30 slogan posters with extremely reactionary contents were discovered on some main streets, the downtown district, and at the gates of some institutions, schools and factories in Kaifeng City....The Kaifeng Public Security Bureau organized nearly 100 cadres and policemen to handle this case. Through nearly five months' hard work, they eventually ferreted out the hidden criminal.

> Criminal Zhao Shujian, male, 33 years of age, is a cadre in the Kaifeng Housing Construction Company. He began to write and put up counterrevolutionary slogans with extremely reactionary contents in 1987. In the spring and summer of this year, when turmoil and a counterrevolutionary rebellion occurred in Beijing, Criminal Zhao took advantage of the opportunity and twice wrote and put up 36 counterrevolutionary posters on 25 April and 20 May [*i.e.*, the day on which martial law was declared in Beijing], thus adding fuel to the flames in the counterrevolutionary rebellion.

> In the interrogation, Criminal Zhao confessed his crimes of writing counterrevolutionary slogans three times, organizing illegal demonstrations, giving counterrevolutionary speeches at Henan University, openly spreading what *Voice of America*

broadcast in his own company, together with other illegal and criminal activities.*

Two points stand out clearly from this classic piece of demagoguery: first, that Zhao Shujian is being persecuted and charged with "counterrevolution" — the most serious crime possible in China, and potentially a capital offense — purely on account of his exercise of the right to free expression; and second, that the release of such prejudicial pre-trial commentary on the case by the authorities, with its manifest presumption of guilt, erases all possibility of Zhao ever receiving a fair trial. Such strongly prejudicial commentary by the authorities is found in virtually all of the Chinese press reports on pro-democracy arrests seen by Asia Watch since last June.

• On December 7, the Changsha Intermediate Court in Hunan Province tried and convicted two workers, Zhang Jingsheng, 35, and Wang Changhuai, 38, on charges relating to their non-violent activities during last year's pro-democracy movement. According to the *Hunan Daily* of December 9, Zhang Jingsheng, a casual laborer in Shaoguan, was sentenced to 13 years imprisonment for making pro-democracy speeches at Hunan University, joining an illegal workers union, writing anti-government leaflets and inciting workers to strike and students to boycott classes.

A *Hunan Radio* broadcast added that Zhang, on May 4 last year, had given a speech at the Changsha Martyr's Memorial calling for the release and rehabilitation of Wei Jingsheng, who was sentenced to 15 years imprisonment in 1979 and is China's best known jailed dissident. A veteran of the Democracy Wall movement himself, Zhang has already spent four years in prison, during the early 1980s, after his conviction on charges of "counter-revolutionary propaganda" for founding and editing a dissident magazine. In true Orwellian vein, the *Hunan Daily* pointed out that Zhang had "continued to have a hostile attitude towards the people after his release."

Wang Changhuai, formerly a worker at the Changsha Automobile Factory, on May 22 joined the recently-set-up Workers Autonomous

---

* In FBIS, December 15, 1989.

14

Federation, quickly becoming head of its organization and propaganda sections. "Awed by the power of policy and law, Wang surrendered to the public security organs on 15 June," according to *Hunan Radio*, and he was given a sentence of three years imprisonment at his trial last December.

- In a significant new development, the authorities recently held secret trials of students detained in the aftermath of the pro-democracy movement. Previously, the great majority of those brought to trial and sentenced since June 4 for their activities during the movement had been either workers or unemployed. According to *Reuters* (December 11, 1989), however, six students from Beijing's College of Foreign Affairs, a prestigious institute for the training of future diplomats, went on trial in November. Requesting anonymity, sources told *Reuters* that four of the students were convicted of "counterrevolution," and the other two on charges of theft; the court imposed punishments ranging from seven to ten years imprisonment. Reportedly, the trials were closed even to the accused's families, and the names of the students are not yet known.

- Between December 1989 and February 1990, dozens of priests, bishops and laymen belonging to the underground Roman Catholic church in northern and western China were arrested, according to several sources. The underground church remains loyal to the Vatican, as opposed to the officially-sanctioned Catholic Patriotic Association, which does not recognize the Pope and which continues to use the Latin mass. In an interview with *Reuters*, the head of the Catholic Patriotic Association stressed that the arrests were political, not religious in nature: to be a member of the underground church was to oppose the government. The wave of arrests may be directly related to the suppression of the pro-democracy movement, as those close to the underground movement reported a surge in the numbers of conversions to Catholicism following the June 4 crackdown.[*]

---

[*]   Reuters, March 2, 1990.

In early February 1990, Politburo member Li Ruihuan assured a foreign journalist that only "about a dozen to 20" intellectuals would eventually be tried and sentenced in connection with the events of last year. Similar official statements have often been made concerning the students. If true, then there can be no justification whatever for the authorities' continued detention of large numbers of students and intellectuals throughout the country, who are not facing trial. They should be freed forthwith. More likely, however, given that secret trials are already known to be underway, is that the great majority of currently detained students and intellectuals are also destined for secret trials, and that only the trials of a very select few will be offered up for public consumption.

Asia Watch has established the identities and documented the circumstances (where known) of more than 500 of those arrested by the Chinese authorities since last June on account of their involvement in the pro-democracy movement. According to all independent estimates, this total represents only a small fraction of the true number of arrests, most of which have never been publicly announced by the authorities. People from virtually all walks of life — students, professors, journalists, artists, engineers, government officials, businessmen and, above all, ordinary workers — have been arrested for their involvement in last year's pro-democracy movement. Many have been accused of committing acts of violence during and after the government's June 3-4 assault on Tiananmen Square. Many others, however, have been accused solely of non-violent activities relating to their free expression of political and other beliefs and on account of their involvement in peaceful protest demonstrations. The majority of those still held have, as far as is known, never been charged at all. The most recent reported arrests were of eight student activists in Lanzhou, north-west China, in early January 1990.[*]

The detainees fall into four broad categories:

First, workers who organized or participated in independent labor organizations that were set up in Beijing and elsewhere in May and early June last year. The most prominent of these groups was the Beijing Workers Autonomous

---

[*]   Agence France Presse, January 8, 1990. In FBIS, same day.

Federation, whose headquarters were sited in the north-west corner of Tiananmen Square. Similar workers' groups, sometimes with very sizeable memberships, appeared in most other major cities in China around the same time. The aim of these independent labor organizations was to provide authentic representation of workers' interests, both economically and politically.

Second, students who played key roles in the formation of such groups as the Beijing Students Autonomous Federation, the Autonomous Federation of Students from Outside Beijing and numerous other independent campus organizations; students who participated in the mass occupation of Tiananmen Square and the week-long hunger strike there; those who organized and ran independent printing presses and published pro-democracy literature of various kinds; and those who acted as liaison links between students in Beijing and in the provinces. Towards the end of the pro-democracy movement, there were at least as many students from the provinces in Tiananmen Square as from Beijing itself; however, because of the present difficulty in obtaining information, the fate of most of those students who made it back to their home towns after June 4 is not known.

Third, leading intellectual figures, journalists, Party theoreticians and college professors, all so-called "black hands" of the movement, whose public statements and writings prior to last spring are said by the authorities to have embodied "bourgeois liberal" thought and hence to have laid the ideological basis for the "counterrevolutionary rebellion" of June 3-4; those who openly sided with the students and workers' cause and who played key roles by organizing large protest demonstrations in Beijing and elsewhere; those who organized such influential groups as the Association for Liaison between All Circles in the Capital; and those who helped coordinate funding for the pro-democracy movement and supplied various kinds of material assistance.

Fourth, the huge numbers of ordinary workers and urban residents, both men and women, who physically confronted the army troops and security forces on the streets of Beijing on the night of the massacre, in a desperate attempt to protect the students in Tiananmen Square; those who helped to shelter fugitive students and workers who had been placed on government wanted lists after June 4; those who took part in demonstrations all over China to protest the crackdown in Beijing;* and those who continued to offer even the slightest

---

* The largest of these protests took place in Chengdu, Sichuan Province, on June 5-6, 1989. Dozens of people were killed by the security forces in the ensuing clashes in the city center.

resistance to the martial law regime — including such things as shouting slogans at troops and holding aloft banners (many of these people were simply shot on the spot) — in the immediate aftermath of the military crackdown.

As can be seen, the scope of the repression is immense. Asia Watch and other organizations have published details of many of those arrested from each of these groups since last June, and some of the more prominent of them are already fairly well known outside of China. They include such people as Wang Dan, the student leader from Beijing University who helped originate the protest movement, and several other student leaders who were placed on the government's "most wanted list," including Liu Gang and Zheng Xuguang; leading establishment intellectuals and theoreticians, such as Bao Tong, the senior advisor to the ousted Party leader Zhao Ziyang; outspoken pro-democracy journalists such as Zhang Weiguo, head of the Beijing bureau of the *World Economic Herald*; Wang Ruowang, a 71-year-old writer who was expelled from the Party along with Fang Lizhi in 1987 following the student demonstrations of the previous winter; and the organizers of China's first independent labor movement since 1949, including Han Dongfang and Liu Qiang, both leaders of the Beijing Workers Autonomous Federation.

None of the above persons has yet been brought to trial or even, so far as is known, formally charged, and all have been held incommunicado since their initial detention. In both these respects, their continued detention — like that apparently of the vast majority of those held by the authorities since the crackdown began — is in violation of the Criminal Procedure Law of China, 1979, and hence unlawful.

The Chinese authorities' arrest and incarceration without trial of these and unknown thousands of other pro-democracy activists and demonstrators constitutes an egregious violation of internationally recognized human rights. The US government should not allow its attention to be diverted from the central fact of these continued mass detentions by such possible impending moves by the Chinese authorities as the selective release of certain of the better-known detainees — or by the granting of permission to Fang Lizhi and his wife, Li Shuxian, to leave China (highly welcome though such measures would be).

Only the granting of a government amnesty to all of those now detained for non-violent expression or association, together with fair and open trials attended by impartial outside observers for all those against whom valid criminal charges can be laid, will suffice as an indication of genuine good faith on the part of the Chinese government. This is what the Reagan administration demanded from the government of Poland as the price for lifting the sanctions imposed by the United States following the imposition of martial law in December 1981, the repression of Solidarity and the arrest of thousands. Indeed, in the case of Poland, the sanctions were not lifted until all the counterparts of China's pro-democracy prisoners were amnestied. In the absence of such an amnesty, selective releases of well-known pro-democracy figures in China can be regarded as no more than a carefully calculated ploy, aimed at fostering an improvement in China's international image and its diplomatic relations with the West.

(ii) Executions

Under Chinese law more than 40 different criminal offenses, notably that of "counterrevolution," may be punished by imposition of the death penalty, and executions are extremely common in China.[*] In 1983, the National People's Congress enacted legislative measures designed to speed up the adjudication of internal security cases and cases involving capital offenses, thereby reducing still further the already woefully inadequate procedural safeguards in Chinese law against the occurrence of wrongful execution. While not actually admitting to the latter, the Chinese legal press has in recent years (that is, the period of relative openness that preceded last June's crackdown) publicized a number of cases in which death sentences had been wrongfully imposed on people solely on the basis of confessions extorted through torture, and where the victims were spared execution only as a result of the fortuitous emergence of the truth or because of frantic last-minute efforts by defense lawyers. According to the official *China Law Daily* of September 5, 1988:

> A particularly serious case occurred [recently] in Anhui Province in which Xie Bingjin, chief of police and former deputy secretary of the Huanggang district Party Committee in Funan County, together with Zhu Gui, the deputy chief of

---

[*]   For example, Hunan Radio announced on December 27, 1989 that 18 criminals had been executed the previous day (FBIS, January 8, 1990); and on January 11, 1990 the China News Service announced the execution the same day of no less than 31 criminals in Canton (Ming Bao January 12, 1990).

police, used torture to extract confessions from suspects. As a result, two people were subsequently given wrongful sentences of death at the trial of first instance, and one person received a suspended death sentence; another was given life imprisonment and ended up being unjustly jailed.

It is likely that many of those executed for alleged violent offenses since June 1989 were in fact innocent, and had given confessions under duress or been convicted on the basis of grossly insufficient evidence. In addition, one man executed in Shanghai in late June, 1989 on charges of setting fire to a train was said to be mentally retarded, and in the widely televised 'trial' proceedings he appeared not to understand what was going on.[*]

The peremptory, almost sly casualness with which the Chinese legal system often seems to regard the question of judicial execution may be seen from the following statement, which is taken from a discussion in an official legal textbook of 1986 regarding the provision in Chinese law that pregnant women are to be exempted from capital punishment.[**] Reveals the author:

> In the view of some [Chinese jurists], if the accused woman is given an abortion prior to the court hearing, then since she will no longer be pregnant by the time the trial began, she can be given the death penalty. And similarly, if the court (sic) performs an abortion on the accused at the time of the trial, then she will likewise become eligible for the death penalty.[***]

In Chinese criminal law, which is held by the authorities to be a "tool of the dictatorship of the proletariat," loopholes are always available when needed.

As mentioned, at least 40 people have already been executed in connection with the events of last June. Many of them had been convicted of crimes involving no use of violence against the person, but only of crimes against property — typically, such things as "burning vehicles" and "setting fire to trains." Others were executed for having allegedly killed martial law troops and

---

[*] Shanghai TV, June 21, 1989; Wenhui Bao, Shanghai, June 21, 1989.

[**] Criminal Law of the PRC, Article 154.

[***] Xin Zhongguo Xingfaxue Yanjiu Zongshu, 1949-1985 (A General Study of Criminological Research in New China), Gao Mingxuan (ed.), Henan People's Publishing House, 1986, p.422.

armed policemen on the night of June 3-4. Some soldiers and police were certainly killed (the government has so far identified only a dozen or so of them, though claiming much higher fatalities) but in at least some of those cases eye-witnesses report that the killings by crowds took place only after the soldiers and policemen had shot and killed unarmed civilians.

In addition, troubling allegations of large-scale extrajudicial executions having been carried out in China continue to surface. Asia Watch was recently informed by a reliable source that, according to a senior official in one of the key central departments of the Chinese Communist Party, "70 secret executions were carried out in Beijing in November [1989]."

A Granada Television documentary screened in Britain late last October contained interviews, filmed secretly inside China, in which Chinese citizens claimed[*] "that since the imposition of martial law thousands have been killed in police raids and executions." Those interviewed also stated: "Students travelling to Fujian and Hebei to spread the news of the massacre [in Beijing] have been unceremoniously killed by local police." In addition: "One family was said to have been offered 4000 pounds sterling (HK$50,000) and access to a new apartment, modern appliances and cheap televisions to keep silent after their son was killed by mistake by the secret police."

Reports of new death sentences and of judicial executions of pro-democracy activists recently carried out still continue to appear in the Chinese press. In view of China's past reporting practices on such matters, moreover, it is likely that those announced in the official press only represent a small portion of the total number of recent executions. The following are some of the cases that have been documented by Asia Watch from Chinese press and radio sources:

- A man named Sun Baohe was executed in Jinan, Shandong Province on October 14, 1989 according to the *Jinan Masses Daily* of the following day. He had been charged only with the crime of having set fire to and burned a "Shanghai-brand" vehicle in the course of a demonstration on June 6.

- Three men — Zhou Qi, He Xiaokang and Chen Guangping — were

---

[*] According to the Hong Kong **South China Morning Post**, October 23, 1989.

executed on November 7, 1989 in Chengdu, Sichuan Province, following their conviction on charges of "beating, smashing, looting and burning" during the period June 4-6. According to Chengdu Radio, the three had attacked the police, engaged in robbery, set fire to a movie theatre and destroyed shops. An official of the Chengdu External Affairs Department stated that they had been publicly paraded at a mass rally and then immediately executed.

- An execution that was carried out in Beijing on November 30, 1989, that of a man named Liu Baode, gives strong cause for concern that pro-democracy activists may have been tried and executed without the true reasons for their execution (namely their involvement in the protest demonstrations of last May and June) actually being made public. An article in the *Beijing Daily* of December 1, 1989 provided a detailed account of several cases of violent crime that had recently been brought to trial, giving the names of those charged, listing their precise criminal activities and stating what the court's sentences on the men had been. All these sentences were of various terms of imprisonment — there were no death sentences imposed.

  The same report, however, stated that Liu Baode, whom it referred to merely as "a hooligan," had been executed by shooting after his sentencing on November 30 by the Beijing Intermediate People's Court. No further details, nor any indication of what the charges might have been, were given. Similarly, the report stated that Su Peng, also "a hooligan," had been sentenced to death with a two-year stay of execution, but again the charges were simply not mentioned. This is unique in Asia Watch's experience of monitoring the Chinese press, and given the particular context of this striking omission, one can only assume that the authorities had something to hide — or rather, that their aim was to 'inform' (the Chinese people) without 'revealing' (to the outside world).

To sum up: the continuing arrests and executions in China form the cutting edge of a protracted, government-led campaign of punitive repression, and they serve a purely political purpose. As Anthony Dicks, an eminent Hong Kong barrister and professor of law at London University, noted recently in *The China*

Quarterly:

> On the afternoon of 4 June 1989...the Supreme People's Court roundly endorsed the counter-revolutionary character of the demonstrations, foreclosing any real possibility of contesting this designation in criminal proceedings in the lower courts....The subsequent arrests and trials of alleged counter-revolutionaries have shown once again how easily the procedural safeguards of the criminal law can be swept aside for the convenience of those in power.*

* "The Chinese Legal System: Reforms in the Balance," The China Quarterly, No.119, September 1989, p.573.

2. PRISON CONDITIONS AND THE USE OF TORTURE

As a result of the clampdown on sensitive information in China today, little specific is known about conditions of detention for those arrested. However, reports that have emerged in recent months indicate that prison conditions are both harsh and brutal. The reports speak of gross overcrowding in cells, severely inadequate diet and widespread infectious diseases — and of frequent beatings and worse.

(i) Conditions of detention

On July 2, 1989, student leader Wang Dan, who topped the government's "most wanted list" after June 4, was arrested in Beijing when he tried to meet secretly with a Taiwan journalist. Both the journalist and his Chinese driver, a man named Wang Yang, were arrested around the same time. The journalist was later released, but Wang Yang was jailed for 45 days. Now in Australia and seeking political asylum, Wang recently told the Hong Kong newspaper *Singtao News* of his conditions of treatment in detention. For the entire 45 days, he said, he was kept shackled by handcuffs and leg-irons, and on each of his daily interrogations by the police he was badly beaten. His cell, a dingy room of only 18 square meters, held no less than 19 prisoners. He explained that he was put on a regime known as "the four dishes and one soup, with permission to wear a watch" — prison jargon which, far from denoting any special privileges, actually meant that his only food was a broth made of four ingredients, and that he had to be kept shackled hand and foot.*

Qincheng Prison, a maximum security facility on the outskirts of Beijing used mainly for the confinement of top political prisoners, is presently reported to contain several hundred student activists and intellectuals from last year's pro-democracy movement. According to the *Washington Post*:

> Chinese sources said that the prisoners in the secretive Qincheng Prison are under psychological pressures common- ly applied to political prisoners. They are denied contact with their families and given political indoctrination courses aimed at getting them to confess to their "errors"....None of these prisoners is accused of engaging in violence. The authorities have apparently not brought formal charges against most of them....Sources say that many of those detained were beaten at the outset of their detention, particularly during the initial interrogation period.**

Conditions at Qincheng are generally believed to be better than in most other prisons in China. On January 2, 1990, however, the Hong Kong newspaper *Ming Bao* published an article based on an interview with a Chinese graduate student, one of the Tiananmen Square hunger strikers, who had recently been released from Qincheng.

According to the student, the majority of those detained at Qincheng bear wounds and injuries inflicted as a result of severe beatings by prison guards, many have given false confessions under duress, and others have become mentally ill. Influenza, lung infections and other diseases were said to be spreading throughout the prison, and "pitiful wailing sounds" could be heard coming from many of the cells. The student added that the interrogation of prisoners was being carried out by the prison guards themselves (this is in fact the norm in China), and that they were being forced to write fresh confessions every day. The student said that he himself had signed an officially prepared statement of confession after being unable to withstand the beatings inflicted upon him, and that he had then been charged with the "crime of deceiving the public security organs" and sentenced to 100 days further detention.

---

* See Shijie Ribao, January 23, 1990.

** Washington Post, October 10, 1989.

Another person detained at Qincheng Prison is Bao Tong, the advisor to Zhao Ziyang. According to one report in the February 20, 1990 edition of the Hong Kong newspaper *Ming Bao*, Bao Tong was being held in solitary confinement, unable to receive visits from family members. The article said he was suffering from malnutrition and that he was not permitted to read newspapers. Asia Watch has not been able to verify the report independently.

On June 2, 1989, as the final act in the student occupation of Tiananmen Square, three leading intellectuals and a well-known popular singer from Taiwan embarked on a 72-hour hunger srike on the monument in the center of the Square. Three of them were subsequently arrested — Liu Xiaobo, Gao Xin and Zhou Duo.* On December 16, 1989, Gao Xin was released, but Liu and Zhou remain behind bars. In early February 1990, Gao Xin broke silence on the time he had spent in prison, and gave an interview to *Associated Press:*

> Gao Xin, a young editor who was denounced by Chinese authorities as a counterrevolutionary plotter, walked out of jail after 185 days — thinner, unemployed and unsure of what life now holds for him...
>
> But in releasing him, authorities didn't say Gao was rehabilitated, forgiven or even cleared. They never formally charged him. Gao said the guards simply told him the investigation into his activities was completed...
>
> When the student crackdown came before dawn June 4, Gao said he and his friends led the students in a peaceful retreat from Tiananmen Square...

Interestingly, the prison guards had "treated Gao with a kind of courtesy not afforded the common criminals in his cell" — an observation consistent with

---

* The singer, Hou Dejian, took refuge in the Australian Embassy; after negotiations with the Chinese government, Hou emerged from the embassy on August 16, 1989, was interviewed by the Chinese media, and now lives relatively freely in Beijing. It appears that he was not arrested at that time because of his willingness to state publicly that there was no massacre in Tiananmen Square itself, a view which accords with the Chinese government's version of events. Asia Watch's representative, Robin Munro, was also present in the Square during the final crucial hours when it was "cleared" of students and workers by the People's Liberation Army, and his eye-witness account (published in South China Morning Post, September 23, 1989, [see FBIS, September 28, 1989] and in Human Rights Watch Newsletter, New York, September 1989) supports Hou's version of events. There was, in fact, no massacre in Tiananmen Square itself, although some killings by troops certainly took place there. The June 3-4 Beijing Massacre, in which somewhere near 1000 citizens were shot or crushed by tanks, took place mainly in the western sector of the city and in the near or immediate environs of Tiananmen Square. To a large extent, it was the leadership shown by the four hunger strikers — Hou, Liu, Gao and Zhou — that persuaded the students to quit the Square minutes before the scheduled military assault on the Monument to the People's Heroes.

other reports that intellectuals, particularly prominent ones, have received much better treatment than detained rank-and-file participants of the pro-democracy movement. The article described Gao's conditions of incarceration as follows:

> He was taken to a small Beijing jail where prisoners were held for short periods before being tried or executed. He shared a 10-square-meter cell with at least seven men at a time, who were accused variously of rape, murder or theft.
>
> Only twice in his six-month stay was he let out for exercise, he said. The cell had a small window, but the heat was overwhelming in late summer. The light was kept burning at night. No books or newspapers were allowed. Four men could sleep on a wooden platform that filled half the cell. Others slept on bedrolls on the floor.
>
> Relatives could not visit. Gao's family was not even told of his arrest. His fiancee went from police station to station seeking news of his whereabouts, but was told each time: "We aren't clear"...
>
> Gao said he was questioned by jail authorities only rarely. He said he was given no clue about his eventual fate. "The loneliness of the spirit was terrible."[*]

The anonymous majority of workers and ordinary urban residents detained since June 4 are believed to be held in local police cells, where torture and other ill-treatment is common, and in various types of so-called "administrative detention centers." The latter are normally used for the confinement of people sentenced solely on police authority, without trial, to short-term periods of imprisonment; legal supervision by outside agencies such as the procuracy is reportedly non-existent in these centers. Every year, many thousands of "offenders" are transferred from such centers, without trial, to serve "administrative sentences" of up to three years' duration in "labor re-education camps," where conditions are reportedly often no less harsh than those in penal colonies proper ("labor reform camps"), which hold court-sentenced criminals.

Chinese press reports have also mentioned the recent use of "shelter and investigation centers" to confine pro-democracy detainees. The purpose of these centers is to hold, for indefinite periods, "suspects" upon whom the police have gathered insufficient evidence of guilt to warrant the issuance of proper

---

[*] Associated Press, February 5, 1990.

criminal charges. Conditions in them are said to be abominable. As one Chinese law journal complained in 1987, in a remarkably candid *exposé*: "At present, there is still no formal legislation concerning shelter and investigation work; nor does such work fall within the orbit of the legal-supervisory organs of the state." The article added: "Some shelter and investigation centers are extremely deficient in terms of health and sanitation conditions, so illness and disease frequently break out in them." Moreover: "Those taken in for shelter and investigation often escape, commit suicide or behave violently."[*]

A Prisoner's testimony

An account just recently obtained by Asia Watch from a pro-democracy detainee who was released in late 1989 and who now resides in a European country, provides us with a rare picture of the general conditions of life in one Beijing detention center where those arrested since last June are currently being held. This account, which describes the treatment of prisoners in a "shelter and investigation center" at No. 21 Paoju Lane, Beijing, is the first really full and detailed one to have emerged from China's prisons since the start of the crackdown. It both confirms the details given in other accounts and also adds a wide range of further information concerning current abuses in Chinese detention centers. Paoju Lane's most famous inmate is Han Dongfang, leader of the Beijing Workers Autonomous Federation (see next chapter for details of Han's imprisonment.)

The informant, a research employee of an institute in Beijing, was arrested without warrant or formal charge in early September 1989 on suspicion of having "concealed guns" after the June 3-4 military crackdown. The police investigation into his case revealed no basis for this allegation, and he was released in late November 1989, along with around 90 others from the same detention center. However, he was first made to sign a statement admitting that he had "violated martial law," an accusation referring to his having merely "stayed on the streets on June 3 and 4...collecting leaflets and taking pictures." Moreover:

> The Public Security Bureau didn't give my work-unit any written document, no explanation for my arrest, nor for my release. So I was arrested without being told why and released

---

[*]   Faxue, (Law Studies), March 1987.

without being told why... The interrogators were not inter-
ested in finding the person who had made the false allegations...

The account confirms reports that intellectuals (and probably students also)
detained since last June are being treated considerably more humanely than
detained workers and others:

I must say objectively that I had a better deal than all the others
in the jail. When the wardens found out my identity they were
very polite and did me some favors so I was comforted slightly.

The following are the key points from his account of detention conditions
in No. 21 Paoju Lane. At the time of his release, the center held approximately
1000 prisoners, half of whom were political prisoners and half of whom were
ordinary criminal offenders. According to the account: "Common criminals and
political prisoners were held together in the same cells." While the Paoju
authorities reportedly were effective in preventing fights between the two
groups, the informant states that in the rest of Beijing: "There were occurrences
of common criminals beating political prisoners in cells in every district of the
city."

In Paoju Lane, the prisoners are crowded into cells like so many cattle. The
former inmate noted that his 14 square meter cell held 23 or 24 people, which
seemed to be standard, as opposed to the pre-June average of about 15 people.
He said prisoners slept on the floor, on bed rolls supplied by their families. The
cells were equipped with a basin and urinal, and the hygiene conditions were
"appalling." He noted that there was a small window which let in some natural
light, and that a single bulb suspended from the ceiling was left on 24 hours.

Because of the severe overcrowding in the cells, most prisoners caught the
skin disease scabies ("hardly anyone avoided this fate"), and they were plagued
by lice ("in the cracks of the floor, the bedding, clothes - lice everywhere"). At
night, sleeping was often impossible:

The floor was always wet. At night, we had to sleep on the floor
so the quilt and cushions were often damp... On average, each
person had only 0.55 square metres floorspace, so everyone
had to squeeze in and be careful how they slept. It was
impossible to lie down flat, everybody had to lie on their sides
and keep the same side till dawn. When we got up we were
aching all over.

Daylight brought little relief from the torment. From reveille at 6.30 a.m. through until bedtime at 9.30 p.m., apart from two meal periods at 10 a.m. and 4.30 p.m., the prisoners had to sit on the floor in four rows of six persons each, without moving or talking. Meals were brought to the cells, and the inmates were allowed out of the cells for only two five-minute trips to the latrines each day. "People were rarely called out to do work. In our cell only one person was summoned to do two days' labor." Access to exercise and fresh-air was scant in the extreme:

> About once or twice a month we were allowed to run around a small yard accompanied by a policeman, and spend 20 minutes moving around... Because I sat without moving for long periods of time, the day after I was released I suddenly felt I couldn't walk, I couldn't move my legs, my knees felt unbearably painful and I had to go to the hospital.

Inevitably, with such severe overcrowding in the cells:

> The air was bad. It stank all day long... I had never realized how precious a thing fresh air is... We urinated in the cells and sometimes even defecated there, because at the toilet times one couldn't always go... The stench was quite often unbearable.

The "no talking" rule was apparently relaxed slightly after National Day, on October 1, and prisoners were sometimes allowed to read *People's Daily* ("one copy between several cells"). However:

> We were not allowed to read books. Even the most basic law books were not allowed... There were no paper or pens in the cells... We were not allowed to write letters to our families, nor could we receive letters from our families... Throughout the period of detention we weren't allowed to meet any relatives, friends or colleagues.

The only 'contact' allowed was via a single postcard (dictated to the prison officer) requesting families to send clothes, bedding, towels, soap, toothpaste and other daily necessities.

The prisoners' diet in Paoju Lane is grossly inadequate, according to the informant. The staple food was *wotou*, a rough steamed bread made of cornflour, with a small quantity of seasonal meat and vegetables added. Most of the former prisoner's fellow inmates lost between five and ten kilograms.

The worst time was just after the crackdown, when a starvation diet was imposed: "In the three months before I was put in the cell, prisoners more or less ate the steamed bread on its own, and the bread was only half-cooked, really horrible to eat." After September 1989, nutritional standards were improved somewhat. (Significantly, this was said by the informant to be partly due to "international protests" which had produced "a certain amount of pressure and some results.") However, *wotou* were often withheld by the wardens as a way of punishing prisoners. In addition: "Food, especially vegetables and meat, were prevented from being given out by the cooking staff. They were not police but they were worse." Starving prisoners who tried to claim extra portions were sometimes beaten and handcuffed by the wardens as a punishment, and one prisoner who tried to hoard food was reportedly shackled for almost ten days.

According to the informant, physical violence against prisoners is less common at Paoju Lane than in other detention facilities in Beijing. For example: "As far as I know, only in Paoju Lane were newly arrived prisoners (when they were put in cells) not beaten by the old prisoners." However:

> If the wardens and interrogators were in a bad mood or if you said something wrong, you would very likely be reprimanded, beaten or sworn at... Some prisoners got beaten up. Torture did happen, but not often.

Other distinctive features of the Paoju Lane detention regime, suggesting that it is considerably better run than is the norm in China, include the fact that interrogations are reportedly carried out by outside officials, rather than by the prison guards themselves. Infringements of prison regulations, however, are dealt with sternly at Paoju:

> Any slight violations were punished. Punishments ranged from standing up for long periods of time to being hand-cuffed... A young political prisoner in my cell was caught by the duty-policeman sharpening a needle with a collar fastener, and he wouldn't admit to it. He was slapped around the face a dozen times by the wardens, and was handcuffed for more than ten days, even whilst eating and going to the toilet. His hands became swollen due to the bad circulation.

Prisoners who fell ill were generally allowed access to the prison doctor. However, medical care was reportedly poor, and medication was issued for one day only: "If this didn't cure the condition, you had to beg to be taken back the next day."

Interrogations were carried out by three-person teams: the interrogator, his deputy and a recorder, with each team being responsible for handling three to five cases.

> If serious, then the interrogations would be frequent, some-times two or three times a day, night and day. If the case was not serious, the interrogations were less frequent. I was only interrogated twice... I did not know the names of my inter-rogators because we weren't allowed to ask.

The interrogations at Paoju produced three categories of prisoners: first, those who were "proven to be guilty and then sentenced"; second, those who (without benefit of trial) were found "guilty of petty crimes" and then sentenced to "a minimum of two years" in "re-education through labor"; and third: "releases...these cases are few."

The informant concludes his account of life in No. 21 Paoju Lane with the comment: "I really tasted what it feels like to be deprived of human dignity. It's unbearable."

(ii) Prevalence of torture: the immediate pre-crackdown period

Torture is far from being a minor problem in China. During an exceptional period of 'judicial glasnost' which began in 1985 and ended last year, the Chinese legal press openly published more than 100 reports exposing several hundred serious cases of torture that had recently been committed by public security and prison officials bent on forcing confessions from criminal suspects. In many of the reported cases, the victims had either died as a result of their ill-treatment or had been left crippled.

Moreover, it appeared from further official statements that the cases revealed were only the tip of the iceberg. According to an article published in the official *China Law Daily* on May 31, 1985:

> The problem is extremely serious in certain areas and units, indeed it has virtually become a "chronic disease", giving the masses the false impression that if one merely enters a public security bureau one will inevitably be beaten. How has it ever been possible for the extracting of confessions through torture to become such a "chronic disease"?

The incidence of torture in police custody showed a steady rise in the second half of the 1980s, particularly in pre-trial detention centers and in the various types of "administrative" holding centers. For example, the 1987 article from *Faxue* magazine, cited above, stated bluntly:

> Administrators and officials in charge of handling case-work in shelter and investigation centers subject the inmates to extensive corporal punishment and abuse, and inflict torture in order to obtain confessions.

The most common forms of torture used by police and other interrogating officials in China include vicious and prolonged beatings, often resulting in damage to the internal organs; applying ropes or handcuffs so tightly to prisoners' wrists that nerves are compressed and blood circulation is stopped, causing extreme pain and sometimes permanent loss of function; and, perhaps most widespread of all, applying electric batons (cattle prods) to various sensitive parts of the body, including the face.

On September 23, 1988, the *Law Daily* described a fairly typical case of torture that had recently taken place in Cangzhou, Hebei Province. Zhu Yongshun, a mentally retarded deaf mute, had been seized by police officers merely for innocently "overhearing" a conversation between them; the man's cousin, Sun Mingdi, then tried to intervene but he too was promptly seized. In the police station the next morning:

> Officer Zhou Linhua first of all tightened up the ropes binding Sun and Zhu, and then began giving the two of them hard karate chops to the back of their necks. The ropes cut deeply into their flesh, causing so much pain that the sweat was soon pouring off of them and their breathing came only in gasps. Officer Sun Xiliang then came across and lashed them both viciously across the ears, and, digging his fingers under the ropes, he placed his knees across their abdomens and forced his weight hard down on top of them. Sun Mingdi lost consciousness there and then.

That evening, the mentally retarded Zhu was sentenced to ten days 'administrative detention' by the police officers. As for Sun Mingdi:

> By 22:00, he was on the verge of death, and had to be taken to the county hospital for emergency treatment. The surgeons extracted 1200 ml. of blood from his abdominal cavity, together with 500 ml. of congealed blood clots, and they

34

excised a 15 cm. length of Sun's small intestine, which had been irreparably damaged. To this day, Sun is still hospitalized.

Another typical case was recounted in *Law Daily* on August 17, 1988 involving a drunk man named Wang Hai'an, who had been detained by police in Zhengzhou, Henan Province on an entirely groundless accusation of "trafficking in children." According to the report:

> Three officers began to interrogate Wang, who had not yet recovered from his state of drunkenness, and to beat and kick him. Officer Mao Yanxi kicked Wang down the stairs, causing him to fall flat on the floor, and he then jumped off a 40 cm. high step directly on to Wang's chest, thereby breaking eight of Wang's ribs. Next, the chief of the police station, Wang Bailing, and Officers Huang Zhihui and Huang Mingxing proceeded to subject Wang to a series of severe beatings. In addition, Officer Mao Yanxi and others struck Wang on the hands and face with their electric batons.

Wang was later released, but on his way home he was suddenly terrified by the sight of three of the policemen pursuing him on a motorbike. Somewhat improbably, the report then states: "Wang thereupon fell into a shallow pool of water and died by drowning."

In addition to physical torture, various kinds of psychological torture are commonly used in Chinese prisons and detention centers — especially for political prisoners. The most ubiquitous form involves endless "study" sessions in which prisoners are forced to internalize the value-system and version of the facts presented to them by the authorities. On his recent release from prison, Gao Xin, one of the Tiananmen hunger strikers, told his fellow hunger striker Hou Dejian of the "very bad treatment" he had endured in prison. "Gao was made to confess his mistakes and express the Communist Party's opinions about what the protests represented and what happened in June," Hou told *Reuters*.[*] Round-the-clock interrogations and denial of all rights to fresh air and exercise are other common forms of psychological torture found in China.

Perhaps the most serious of all, however, is the use of prolonged solitary confinement. Wei Jingsheng has been held in solitary since his conviction in 1979, and is thought to have developed schizophrenia as a result. Another

---

*   <u>Reuters</u>, January 9, 1990.

leading figure from the Democracy Wall period, Xu Wenli, has also been held in solitary in Beijing No.1 Prison ever since his sentence to 15 years imprisonment in 1982. After the smuggling out and publication abroad of his prison notes in 1985, Xu was for several years confined in a tiny, windowless cell to which the only access was through a trapdoor located in the ceiling. When a reporter from the *South China Morning Post* visited Beijing No.1 Prison in September, 1989 she was told by the vice-warden, Song Wenbo, that Xu Wenli was still in solitary confinement. Solitude, declared Song, was "beneficial to Xu's individual reform."[*]

Despite a prolonged campaign from 1985 onwards by the authorities to eradicate the use of torture in China, the *Law Daily* nonetheless noted on September 5, 1988 that there had been "a constant increase" in the incidence of physical torture and other types of rights-violation over the past two years. And as Anthony Dicks recently observed, regarding the televised trials of "counterrevolutionaries" in China last summer:

> Scenes of prisoners being humiliated and manhandled as they were paraded before the courts for sentencing...were a reminder to the world of how flimsy are the legal safeguards against torture and physical abuse of prisoners in China.[**]

In view of the drastic deterioration in the general standard of human rights observance that has occurred in China since the government crackdown of June 1989, there is strong reason to believe that the incidence of serious torture in police custody is now higher than ever.

---

[*]   South China Morning Post, September 1, 1989.

[**]   Op cit, p.574.

3. SUPPRESSION OF THE WORKERS MOVEMENT ("THE POLISH DISEASE")

The pro-democracy movement of 1989 was initiated by the students, through their mass occupation of Tiananmen Square and through the week-long hunger strike they conducted there. But at its height, the movement commanded active support from virtually all sectors of society, and particularly from the workers. By the end of May, independent labor organizations had sprung up spontaneously in numerous other major cities in China, including Shanghai, Nanjing, Changsha, Xi'an, Hangzhou, Guizhou and Wuhan. This posed a formidable challenge to the Communist Party authorities, whose legitimacy rests upon their claim to be "the vanguard of the proletariat."

Not surprisingly therefore (although this has largely gone unnoticed in the West), it is the workers in China who have in fact borne the brunt of the recent and continuing repression. They form the great majority of those who have been detained, their conditions of detention ("30 to a cell," according to *UPI*)[*] are much harsher than those of other groups, and they have been handed down exemplary prison sentences by the courts. They are also the ones most likely to be subjected to torture and other forms of gross ill-treatment during police interrogation. Significantly, all those known to have been executed since June 4 were either workers or unemployed.

The unsung nature of the independent labor movement in China is well illustrated by the fate since last June of Han Dongfang, 26-year-old leader of the Beijing Workers Autonomous Federation (BWAF). Han, a railway main-

---

[*]   UPI, in South China Morning Post, November 5, 1989.

37

tenance worker who deserves to be better known as "China's Lech Walesa," has been held in secret incommunicado detention by the authorities in Beijing ever since late June, 1989. Although his name, like those of the main student leaders from Tiananmen Square, such as Wang Dan and Wu'erkaixi, topped the government's "most wanted" lists just after the massacre in Beijing, the authorities have never announced or made public the fact of Han's arrest. According to sources inside the public security service, Han Dongfang is now gravely ill. Unable to hold down any food, he has just been hospitalized for the sixth time and is currently on an intravenous drip.

Further detailed information on Han's condition has just recently become available, through the remarkable account — cited in the previous chapter — of life in Paoju Lane detention center, where Han has been incarcerated since last June. According to the account:

> At first, Han Dongfang was kept in a large cell like the other political prisoners. But because he wouldn't admit to any mistakes and used to talk provocatively, he was later kept in "isolation." Han had a stomach problem in and around July, due to the summer heat and poor food. The trouble started up again. At first, the police thought that he was pretending and wouldn't take him to the doctor. He was very depressed. After other cell-mates begged on his behalf, the police agreed to take him.

> He took the opportunity to shout out in the corridor: "How pitiful we Chinese are! We don't even respect our own kind. I wouldn't want to be a Chinese again in my next life." He shouted his head off and refused to go to the hospital. "I swear I'll never ask to see the doctor again. I'll be damned if I will!" Then he returned to his cell. His shouting was heard by all the prisoners in the second-floor cells. Everyone was very agitated and felt very sympathetic towards Han for the unjust treatment he was receiving. Many of them shed tears.

38

The police got scared, and the prison governor himself brought a doctor to see Han. Shortly afterwards, however, they put him into the "Small Cell" [a tiny isolation cell used for punishment purposes], separating him from all the other prisoners.

The Beijing Workers Autonomous Federation (BWAF) was formed by Han Dongfang and a small number of other workers on May 19, the eve of the declaration of martial law. Apart from a small, short-lived workers group that was set up in Taiyuan, Shanxi Province in the winter of 1980, the BWAF is thought to have been the first truly independent labor organization in China since the founding of the People's Republic. Based in two small tents set up in the northwest corner of Tiananmen Square, the BWAF was a fledgling organization, but it appears to have enjoyed wide support from within key sections of the Beijing workforce. Through its small broadcasting station on the Square, the organization gave out nightly programs of news, commentary and political analysis, attracting enthusiastic audiences of several thousands, sometimes until dawn.

In its *Provisional Outline*, adopted in the Square on May 28, 1989, the BWAF made clear its intention to operate openly and in full conformity with the laws and constitution of the PRC. The main aims and principles of the BWAF were as follows:

> The Federation shall be an entirely independent and autonomous organization, built up by the workers on a voluntary basis and through democratic processes; it should not be subject to control by other organizations.

---

*   A book entitled The Great Prisons of Western China ("Zhongguo Xibu Da Jianyu", published by the Jiangsu Literature and Art Publishing House in September 1986) gives the following graphic description of the nature and uses of China's notorious "Small Cells" (Xiao Hao): "Every prison has its 'Small Cell'. This is a room of two or three square metres in area, with a steel door carrying a small aperture which provides the only source of light. Apart from a small bed, there is nothing in the room at all. It is like a single guest-room for convicts. Living in it, one suffers from neither sunshine, wind nor sand. But after a few days, one turns all white and pasty... The 'Small Cell' is certainly no guest house. It is an operating table for felons. Loneliness is the scalpel, used for performing surgery upon the souls of those overly fond of fun and excitement....Only the most outstanding police officers know how to use their electric baton and the 'Small Cell' to best effect." The book then describes the effect of the "Small Cell" upon a prisoner who spent only a few days in one: "Day 1: They lock him up in the 'Small Cell' for a spell of forced introspection...; Day 2: He's still lying on the bed, feeling quite happy. Day 3: He feels a little lonely... Day 4: He starts to feel rather afraid. The ray of light piercing the little aperture has been mercilessly halved in size by a steel bar. The room is like some dim cave. Day 5: He is plunged into terror. The ghostly shadows of loneliness play over the four white walls all around, seeming to grin hideously at him. He involuntarily breaks out in a cold shiver. He screams insanely and bangs on the steel door. He jumps up and down on the bed, and then starts rolling around underneath it. Over the next few days, he begins to repent."

The founding principle of the Federation shall be to address the political and economic demands of the workers, and it should not serve merely as a welfare body.

The Federation shall perform the role of monitoring the party of the proletariat — the Chinese Communist Party. Within the bounds of the law and constitution, it shall strive to protect all legal rights of its members.

On June 2, 1989 the BWAF was declared by the authorities to be a "counterrevolutionary" organization. The federation's tents were to be the first target of attack by the massive PLA force which arrived at the Square in the early hours of June 4, and many of its members were hunted down and arrested in the weeks and months thereafter. The day before the massacre in Beijing, Han Dongfang said:

We fully expect the authorities to take action against us. We've taken certain precautions. But if they use violence against us, well, we are unarmed and we will not resort to the use of violence against them. We are prepared to go to prison, and we are not afraid to die. I only hope that the international community will rally to our defense if the government does try to suppress us.

The reason for the unaccustomed discretion shown by the authorities, in their failure publicly to reveal the fact of Han's arrest, is plain enough. For China's leaders are above all concerned to prevent the emergence of what they refer to as the "Polish disease" — namely, organized industrial unrest. Just after the declaration of martial law on May 20, Han Dongfang's BWAF proposed a general strike in support of the students in the Square. Had it transpired, Deng Xiaoping and his colleagues might now be collecting their retirement pensions — or worse.

4. DEFECTS OF THE CRIMINAL JUSTICE SYSTEM

Perhaps the most important human rights concern in China today is the question of what is going to happen to all the thousands of people currently being held in police detention. Since most of them will probably be brought to trial eventually, it is worth examining in some detail the nature of the judicial system through which they must pass. Without doubt, China's criminal justice system is among the most deeply flawed in the world — indeed, it is essentially pre-modern.

First, there is no such thing as the presumption of innocence in China. The Chinese legal system, going against both the spirit and the letter of the Universal Declaration of Human Rights, explicitly rejects the principle that a detained person should be presumed innocent until proven guilty. In its place, judicial officials are blandly instructed merely "to take facts as the basis and use law as the yardstick" when handling criminal suspects. The argument given is that to presume people's innocence would be to prejudge the issue, and would mean that China's police would never be justified in arresting anyone at all.

Thus, although China claims not to presume guilt, the first thing detainees see when they enter police cells is a large sign on the wall saying: "lenience to those who confess, severity to those who resist."* Penitence is essential, and any attempt to argue innocence is generally taken as evidence of a "bad attitude" and as further proof of guilt. This stress on the importance of the prison

---

* The guidelines set by Ren Jianxin, President of the Supreme People's Court, for handling the trials of pro-democracy demonstrators forcefully reiterated this time-honored 'principle' of Chinese law: "In the course of adjudication, we must combine punishment with leniency. We must deal with those who confess their crimes with leniency and inflict severe punishment on those who refuse to do so." (Beijing Television, July 15, 1989; in FBIS, July 17, 1989)

confession accounts, in turn, for the authorities' frequent recourse to the baleful rituals of torture. Releases or acquittals are rare, for they imply that the judicial officers concerned have made some mistake, and this brings loss of face.

Second, the system of legal defense is woefully inadequate. Criminal detainees are expressly denied access to a lawyer throughout the period of pre-trial custody and interrogation, and may only seek legal counsel once the indictment has been issued and the case is ready to go to court — which is usually no more than two to three days before the start of trial. This more or less ensures that the lawyer has insufficient time in which to gather evidence and prepare a proper case. It also means that throughout the crucial period of the police interrogation, detainees have no-one at hand to advise them of their rights or to ensure that they are not ill-treated, beaten or tortured.

In addition, lawyers are subjected to blatant political control and inter-ference in the execution of their duties. According to an article in *Faxue* (Law Studies) magazine in February 1988:

> Some local justice departments have a regulation that if a lawyer wants to present a defense of "not guilty" in a criminal case, then he must first of all obtain permission from the Party organization of the justice department concerned.

Evidently, the political authorities in China are even able to prevent defendants from trying to plead innocent.

Fourth, not only is there no independence of the judiciary in China (since judges are answerable to Party-dominated "adjudication committees" and "politics and law committees"), but the verdicts themselves are usually decided upon before the trial even begins. In fact, this unique system of justice - known in China (as in the topsy-turvy world of *Alice in Wonderland*) as "verdict first, trial second" — is openly acknowledged to be the norm. As the Shanghai magazine *Minzhu Yu Fazhi* (Democracy and Law) explained in July 1988:

> Our current trial practice in all cases, regardless of whether they are major or minor, criminal, civil, economic or ad-ministrative ones, is that the adjudication committee must first give its opinion on what the appropriate ruling should be, and this is then implemented [in court] by the panel of judges.

Continued the article:

> 'Verdict first, trial second' is tantamount to walking along a

road on the top of one's head: it violates the law of proper procedure...."Brilliant luminaries," who have not carried out any investigations or even read the case dossier, but have instead merely listened to an oral report on the case, are allowed to make the ruling in advance [of the trial]. Even if they reach an erroneous verdict, the panel of judges must submit to it completely and unconditionally; there is no room allowed for debate or disagreement.

And finally:

The practice of "verdict first, trial second" can easily give rise to serious miscarriages of justice....It gives the green light to those who seek to put their own word before the law....It deprives the parties of their right of appeal....It reduces the whole series of legally-established procedures and principles to the level of an empty formality. All such things as "public trial," "the judges panel," "people's assessors," "legal defense" and "withdrawal" are stripped of all practical meaning and significance.

The prevalence of such practices demonstrates the full and bitter irony of the Chinese authorities' claim to be pursuing the current crackdown against dissent "strictly in accordance with the rule of law." For in reality, the 'rule of law' in China today is a one-edged sword which can only cut downwards. The criminal justice system has always operated at the whim of the political authorities, but since last June it has been used as a direct instrument of wholesale political repression. So far as the many thousands of imprisoned Chinese supporters of democracy now awaiting trial are concerned, there is simply no rule of law in China worth mentioning, and no justice can be expected.

5. SUPPRESSION OF FREEDOM OF EXPRESSION

> The Monument to the People's Heroes is surrounded with chains, and tourists are not allowed to set foot on the steps. On the four sides of the monument stand wooden notices about one square meter in size, on which are inscribed the regulations to be observed in paying respects to the monument. One of the regulations forbids any painting, drawing, inscribing, posting, hanging and placing of any slogans, big- or small-character posters, or any other propaganda materials in any form. Anybody who wishes to lay wreaths at the monument must seek approval from the duty personnel, and the wreaths must be laid at designated spots.
>
> > (report of the official *China News Service*, on January 11, the day of the lifting of martial law)*

The enchainment of the monument in the centre of Tiananmen Square, where the students made their last stand in the early hours of June 4, 1989 aptly symbolizes the state of freedom of expression in China as a whole as the country enters the new decade. The domestic press, which had shown signs of supporting the pro-democracy cause last spring was comprehensively muzzled at the outset of the crackdown, and it still remains so; fresh restrictions upon foreign journalists, deftly replacing those imposed under Martial Law Order No.3, have just been issued by the authorities; stringent censorship regulations are being passed in various cities, simultaneously banning "anti-socialist writings" and

---

* In <u>FBIS</u>, January 12, 1990.

"obscene literature"; and a nationwide purge of publishing houses is fast getting under way. Regulations restricting the formation of "social organizations" have been rushed into force, and the authorities (showing a previously unsuspected sense of humor) have even chosen recently to promulgate China's first-ever law on "freedom of assembly and demonstration."

The continued maintenance by the Chinese authorities of their false version of what actually happened last May and June has required strenuous efforts in the realm of press control. Jiang Zemin, the Party's general secretary, last November summed up the regime's main charge against the news media as follows:

> We must be soberly aware that the ideological trend of bourgeois liberalization has run unchecked in the past few years and led to the turmoil and counterrevolutionary rebellion at the turn of spring and summer this year. This has exposed many problems, some very serious, in media circles. Instead of exposing and criticizing bourgeois liberalization and stopping the turmoil, certain media units provided a forum for the instigators and supporters of the turmoil and rebellion, thus stirring up the turmoil and adding fuel to the flame of the rebellion. This has caused great ideological confusion among the masses.

In a generous mood, Jiang then went on to spell out — though quite unintentionally — the true meaning and content of the Party's concept of press freedom in China:

> Certainly, requiring propaganda and mass media to maintain political unity with the Party Central Committee propaganda does not mean mechanical parroting of political slogans. Rather, it requires them to keep to the stand of the Party and people and, by way of diverse forms, to accurately and vividly reflect and instill the Party's political standpoint, principles and policies into news stories, newsletters, commentaries, photos, headlines and layout.*

After the June 4 crackdown, propaganda officers of the PLA took over control of all the main newspapers in Beijing, and editorial departments were thoroughly overhauled. Qin Benli, chief editor of *Shijie Jingji Daobao* (World

---

* "Jiang Zemin gives speech on mass media work," New China News Agency, November 29, 1989; in FBIS, December 7, 1989.

Economic Herald), the outspokenly pro-reform Shanghai newspaper, had been sacked even before the crackdown, and his Beijing deputy editor, Ruan Jianyun, was arrested last October. Yu Haocheng, former director of the Masses Publishing House (the organ of the public security authorities) and a leading advocate of legal reform, was arrested sometime last summer; and Yang Hong, a journalist on the *China Youth Daily*, has been detained since June 13 on charges of circulating "rumor-mongering leaflets" and protesting against corruption. Eighteen other journalists or editors are known to have been arrested, but the true figure is probably much higher.

Many editors in China have been making strenuous efforts to shield and protect their journalists from the authorities' continuing purge of "unreliable media elements." Latest reports indicate, however, that a high-level decision has now been made to remove these editors themselves, so that the purge may proceed more smoothly. On January 13, 1990 *Reuters* reported the recent sacking of Guan Zhihao, director of *Law Daily* (and a prime architect of the post-1985 period of "judicial glasnost" referred to earlier), and also that of Xie Yongwang, liberal-minded editor of the Shanghai journal *Literature and Arts*. According to *Reuters*, the two have been sacked for seeking to protect their journalists from government retribution and for publishing articles last summer supportive of the students' demands.

On January 20, the Hong Kong newspaper *Ming Bao* reported that the CPC Propaganda Department had issued an order sometime after New Year calling for a renewed and intensified purge of the news media, so that editors who had failed to fall into line after June 4 could be replaced and the "cleaning out" of journalistic ranks could begin properly. Mu Qing, director of the *New China News Agency*, and Zhou Bingde, deputy director of *Voice of China* and the niece of Premier Zhou Enlai, head the list of senior press officials about to be sacked, according to the report.

Next in line for official "cleansing" is the publishing world as a whole. On December 6, 1989, the *New China News Agency* reported that the Press and Publications Administration of China had decided to abolish or suspend the licenses of 10 percent of all existing publishing houses: "Newspaper and magazine offices which publish pornographic stories or articles which run counter to the Party's line will be deprived of their licences." On January 11, 1990, the agency revealed that the Press and Publication Administration had issued a circular requiring all publishing houses to register anew between

January 15 and the end of the month. "The circular points out that in recent years publications with serious political errors and obscene and violent content have appeared despite repeated prohibitions."[*]

The precise meaning of the terms "anti-socialist" and "reactionary," as applied to writing and literature in China, have been formally codified by the authorities in recent weeks. According to Article 4 of the *Temporary Provisions of the Shanghai Municipality on the Banning of Harmful Publications*, enacted on November 26, 1989:

> Reactionary publications refer to those opposing the people's democratic dictatorship and the socialist system, and include publications containing one of the following contents:
>
> 1. Opposing the Communist Party of China and its leadership.
>
> 2. Attacking the People's Republic of China and opposing taking the socialist road.
>
> 3. Attacking and vilifying the people's democratic dictatorship.
>
> 4. Denying the guiding position of Marxism-Leninism and Mao Zedong Thought.
>
> 5. Seriously distorting historical facts, advocating division of the state and people, and vilifying the Chinese people.[**]

The penalties for infringing these regulations range from a maximum fine of 30,000 *yuan* to criminal prosecution and unspecified terms of imprisonment.

Finally, on December 22, 1989 senior legislators meeting in Beijing to discuss a new draft law on authors' rights stated that henceforth "any anti-socialist and anti-communist works should be banned in China." According to the *New China News Agency*: "The basic principle of anti-bourgeois liberalization should be spelled out in the draft...and the rights of authors who produce anti-socialist and anti-communist works should never be protected."[***]

The vitriolic outpourings of criticism against the Western media, and especially that of the US, continue as before for domestic audiences, although

---

[*]   New China News Agency, in FBIS, January 11, 1990.

[**]   Jiefang Ribao, December 5, 1989; in FBIS, January 10, 1990.

[***]   New China News Agency, December 22, 1989; in FBIS, December 27.

they are now less prominent in the externally-directed media. In a sustained diatribe against the evils of Western-style "news authenticity," for example, an article of last December declared:

> The "Voice of America," which has always claimed to be "objective and just," has been condemned by the people of the world and regarded as a "rumormonger." The "news authenticity" which the bourgeoisie has bragged about has been seen through by more and more people.

To drive home its main thesis — the essential duplicity of the Western press — the article cited (inappropriately enough) the Watergate Affair:

> For example, the world-shaking "Watergate Scandal" revealed by the *Washington Post* and other newspapers and journals was a farce which reflected the open strife and veiled struggle between the financial groups in the eastern and western parts of the United States.

In light of this essentially conspiratorial view of the foreign press, it is perhaps small wonder that only nine days after the lifting of martial law in Beijing the authorities should have seen fit to impose a fresh set of regulations on the news-reporting activities of foreign journalists, to replace those imposed as part of the post-June 4, 1989 clampdown. The new regulations ban all articles by foreigners that in the authorities' view "distort facts" or "violate the public interest," and journalists may be expelled if faulted on these counts. As was the case under the martial law rules, foreign journalists are prohibited from conducting interviews with any "work unit" unless prior approval has been obtained from the authorities, and they may not deviate from the agreed program.[**] As one Western diplomat commented, regarding the new press regulations for foreigners: "If they feel like it, they can get you on whatever they want." Noted another: "In real terms, nothing has changed."[***]

In addition, restrictions on access by Chinese people to foreign television

---

[*] FBIS, December 19, 1989.

[**] There are even signs that the English language itself is now considered to be subversive. Beijing's highly popular "English Corner," where Chinese of all ages used to come to practise their conversation, was just recently closed down by the authorities. According to the New York Times of December 19, 1989: "In mid-November, the area was cordoned off and notices went up, saying, 'English Corner has been withdrawn.' The university teachers, the notices said, no longer had the time."

[***] Reuters, January 20, 1990; New York Times, January 21; and Shijie Ribao, January 22.

broadcasts have also been imposed recently. According to the *Hong Kong Standard*, a municipal directive was issued by the authorities in Canton on January 1, 1990 banning the installation in the city of aerials capable of receiving television signals from outside of China. This ends a 10-year period during which the residents of Canton have been able to watch Hong Kong television programs freely. As a local cadre commented in the report: "The authorities obviously want to stop people from being influenced by overseas reports on important issues, including the dramatic upheavals in Eastern Europe."[*]

News censorship has been heavily evident in China throughout the recent events in Eastern Europe. Mandarin-language broadcasts of both the Voice of America and the British Broadcasting Corporation have been jammed by the authorities, and China's own press coverage of the major political turnarounds in the Eastern Bloc has been tightly controlled. Radical political change and moves towards democracy in the Eastern Bloc countries have been presented as being mainly the result of elite leadership decisions, rather than public pressure, and as constituting steps "to perfect socialism" and ensure "stability and unity."[**] More generally, the upheavals in Eastern Europe have been presented by the Chinese authorities as merely proving their claim that the West is applying a "capitalist strategy of peaceful evolution" against the socialist world.[***]

As mentioned above, a series of laws and regulations governing Chinese citizens' rights of assembly, demonstration and association have been enacted in recent months and weeks. The net effect of these is to restrict still further the almost negligible prospects for free assembly, demonstration and association in

---

[*]   *Hong Kong Standard*, January 6, 1990.

[**]   *New York Times*, December 24, 1989.

[***] *New York Times*, December 22, 1989. The charge that the West is trying to make China "peacefully evolve into a bourgeois republic" was first made by Deng Xiaoping, directly after the June 4 massacre. As the *People's Daily* explained on December 1, 1989: "The international reactionary forces...will work in coordination with the turmoil created in socialist countries in an attempt to force them to make concessions to them so that socialist countries may 'peacefully evolve' into capitalist countries, thus turning those socialist countries into their vassal states. Imperialists have openly declared that their principle is to implement political pluralism and market economy in socialist countries; in other words, they want to implement the bourgeois multiparty system and rotatory term of office, while driving the Communist Party out of office and eventually restoring capitalism."

China, by formalizing the role and prerogatives of the state authorities in the regulation of these various types of civil activity. In the case of the *Regulations on the Registration of Social Organizations*, issued by the State Council in October, 1989 for example, it is clear that a primary purpose of the document is to render unlawful any future formation of the kinds of student and worker organizations which sprang up all around the country last May and June. Commenting in November on the issuance of the new regulations, Fan Baojun, the Vice-Minister of Civil Affairs, in effect compared these pro-democracy organizations to the Chinese Triads:

> There are an estimated 100,000 local community groups in the country. But there are some problems with these... Moreover, some secret societies or underworld gangs that existed before 1949 have been revived in some backward and coastal areas. Some illegal organizations have already caused severe damage to the State and the Party, such as the "Autonomous Student Union of Beijing Universities," which stirred up "counterrevolutionary" rebellion in Beijing last spring.

The *Law of the PRC on Assemblies, Parades and Demonstrations*, adopted on October 31, 1989, is also clearly aimed at preventing the re-emergence of any sign or inkling of the kinds of mass public activity seen last summer in Beijing. Among other things, the law prohibits citizens from "starting or organizing assemblies, parades or demonstrations in cities where they are not residents, nor shall they participate in activities held by the local people"; and it forbids foreigners from taking part in all such activities without prior permission from the authorities. The police are granted sweeping powers to determine all aspects of any assemblies and demonstrations. In addition, the law pointedly bans all unauthorized parades and demonstrations within a 300-meter radius of a series of government institutions in central Beijing, the effect of which is to make it unlawful for any future protest demonstrations to be held in Tiananmen Square. Penalties of up to five years imprisonment are laid down for those who violate

---

* China Daily, November 1, 1989; in FBIS, same day.

the law.[*] On January 9, the Shanghai municipal authorities adopted a set of regulations for the law's specific enforcement, and the Beijing authorities did likewise on January 12, the day after martial law was lifted.[**]

One would think that such comprehensively restrictive measures, when viewed in the light of the current repression as a whole, would surely suffice to deter most potential "counterrevolutionaries" from even trying to demonstrate openly. Astonishingly, however, it seems that Chinese workers and students have in fact been flocking to the authorities in the hundreds of thousands in recent months, in order to test the value of the new laws' promises regarding freedom of association and the right to demonstrate.

According to the *New York Times* of January 8, 1990 for example:

> Party sources said groups representing thousands of workers across the country who have been suffering under the government's economic austerity program, which has reduced inflation but brought the country to the brink of recession, have sought permission to air their grievances.

Moreover:

> The *South China Morning Post*...reported last week that workers in more than 30 Chinese cities had applied to carry out legal demonstrations involving a total of more than 500,000 workers. Party sources could not confirm the figure of 500,000, but said worker discontent was widespread and involved most of the country's provinces.

Clearly, the "Polish disease" has already gone well past the merely incubatory stage in China today. The response of the Chinese authorities to these polite requests for the observance of their rights by workers was, however, predictably churlish:

> According to the sources, the leadership issued an order to security forces that they use 'whatever force is necessary' to crush any demonstrations staged by workers.

The full shock-waves of the recent events in Eastern Europe are, of course, still to come.

---

[*] Text of the law is in FBIS, November 1, 1989.

[**] FBIS, January 10, 1989; Shijie Ribao, January 13, 1989.

6. HARASSMENT OF CHINESE STUDENTS IN THE U.S.

Frankly speaking, the United States was involved too deeply in the turmoil and counterrevolutionary rebellion that occurred in Beijing not long ago.

(Deng to Nixon, November 1989)[*]

For the more than 40,000 Chinese students now living and studying in the US, the past nine months or so have been a time of deep anxiety and insecurity. Although insulated for the present from the full traumatic impact of China's continuing campaign against the twisted proponents of "bourgeois liberalism" and the cringing residues of last year's "counterrevolutionary rebellion," many of them know that they are but a plane ticket away from an unenviably vulnerable position at the front line. Over the past decade, the Chinese leadership has waged a protracted struggle to try to stem the rising tide of so-called "spiritual pollution" from the West, culminating in the recent all-out war in China against "bourgeois liberalism," its political twin. These two phenomena – the 'Tweedledum and Tweedledee' of Dengist demonology – are viewed by the present Chinese leadership as being essentially American in origin. For this reason, Chinese who come here to study must be carefully monitored, lest they transport the 'problem pair' back to China with them on their return.

Several of the ways in which this monitoring of Chinese students has been carried out by the authorities since June 4, 1989, however, amount under US

---

[*] <u>Washington Post</u>, November 1, 1989.

law to serious harassment and restriction of the right to free expression. In the immediate aftermath of the crackdown, Chinese Embassy staff were widely reported to have been videotaping students who took part in protest demonstrations and issuing them with veiled threats by telephone concerning the safety of their relatives back home.[*]

In late September, 1989 more such reports were heard as Chinese students prepared to carry out nationwide protest demonstrations on October 1, China's national day. According to the *New York Times*, "They [Chinese Embassy officials] have been calling students nationwide and threatening them...Chinese students [have] been told that their passports might not be extended and that their relatives back home might suffer if the students expressed support for China's democracy movement." Jack Brooks, chairman of the House Judiciary Committee, added that the Chinese Government was "keeping blacklists of pro-democracy students here in America." And according to a report prepared in September by the recently-formed Independent Federation of Chinese Students and Scholars: "The Chinese Embassy and its consulates around the country have dramatically stepped up their efforts to intimidate Chinese students."[**]

The Chinese authorities have been particularly concerned at the formation overseas in recent months by Chinese nationals of a number of quite large and well-organized opposition groups, in particular the Paris-based Federation for a Democratic China, which has offices in several cities in the US. Recent press reports assert that the Chinese authorities have begun dispatching teams of security agents to monitor the activities of these overseas groups and to ascertain their Chinese student memberships.[***]

---

[*]   Washington Post, June 14, 1989; Hong Kong Standard, June 14, 1989.

[**]   New York Times, September 27, 1989.

[***] See for example Shijie Ribao, January 19, 1990; and Taipei Central News Agency, December 15, 1989, in FBIS December 19, 1989.

A common reprisal reportedly being taken by Chinese consular officals against students who participated in last year's protest demonstrations in the US, or who for example resigned their Party memberships in protest at the crackdown, is to refuse to extend their passports upon expiration. According to the Independent Federation of Chinese Students and Scholars, "more than 100" and possibly "as many as 400 or 500" such cases have occurred recently.[*]

The complaint most widely voiced by Chinese students in the US, however, is that their mail is being routinely interfered with by the authorities in China. According to the results of a survey carried out recently by Congressman Benjamin A. Gilman,[**] more than 92% of Chinese student respondents said that their mail either to or from China had been intercepted, delayed or tampered with in some way by the Chinese authorities. In certain cases, this harassment had been extended to their families in China as well, in the form of visits and threats from public security officials regarding the content of letters they had received.

Asia Watch recently received the following account written by a Chinese student in the US. We reproduce it here in full, for it vividly conveys both the nature of the abuse and the sense of outrage felt — and also the taste of a victory won which, though small, seems somehow to catch the essence of the present struggle for human rights in China.

> June 8, 1989. I sent a letter to my mother and brothers, which had contents about the 'June 4' massacre. My family received it at the end of June. My family is in Xi'an township, Taoyuan County, Hunan Province.
>
> July 13. In the morning, two public security agents went into my village to investigate. In the afternoon, my third brother (who had highest education in my village except me: elementary school graduate) was ordered to go to the township government to submit my letter. My brother refused. Four officials interrogated him from afternoon to the night. At about 1:30am after midnight, my brother gave in.
>
> October 6. I knew part of the facts. I wrote a letter to the

---

[*]   Shijie Ribao, November 30, 1989.

[**]   "A History of the deliberate interference with the flow of mail: The cases of the Soviet Union and the People's Republic of China," a report by Rep. Benjamin Gilman, Chairman on Postal Operations and Services, submitted to the Committee on Post Office and Civil Service of the US House of Representatives on November 9, 1989.

Hunan Public Security Bureau and the PRC Embassy in Washington. I asked the government to return my letter and apologize to my family, because they violated Article 40 of the "PRC Constitution," which protect the freedom and privacy of citizens' correspondence. I also cited words from Chinese government, which repeatedly promised that overseas Chinese students will not be punished for their participation in democracy movement. I said I will publish this story two months later if they do not respond. A copy of this letter was sent to the PRC Consulate in Chicago.

I received a letter from the Chicago Consulate. They said they knew nothing about this case before receiving my letter. They had written to the Hunan Public Security Bureau and the Embassy in Washington and asked the government to deal with this case seriously.

November 16. I knew more facts and wrote to the government in my township. A copy of this letter was sent to Hunan Public Security Bureau, PRC Embassy, and Chicago Consulate.

I received a message. The government has not yet returned my letter but instead on November 16 investigated my brothers and sisters and my previous letters to them. The officials asked my brother to transfer a message to me: Do not make a hard time to the government.

If the government do not return my letter to my family, I will publish the story in news media in a few months. The title will be: "In Mainland China, son does not have freedom to write to his mother." In order for China to have democracy, we need to fight within the system. If more Chinese fight for their rights, China has hope. Protecting individuals' rights could be more important than protesting or demonstrating in some instances. From November I only need two weeks to receive letter from my family, which is in a remote mountain area (before it took four weeks).

7. TIBET: ABUSES UNCHECKED

Arrests, trials and torture continue as before in Tibet. Martial law, imposed in Lhasa on March 7, 1989, may well have been the model for what took place in Beijing just three months later. The use of excessive force on June 4 to suppress non-violent demonstrators based in Tiananmen Square has even been seen by some observers as the "Tibetanization" of Beijing. The human rights abuses in Lhasa before and after demonstrations there in March were a virtual laboratory for what came later to students, workers, intellectuals and ordinary citizens in the Chinese capital. In fact, had there been sufficient international attention and protests against the shooting, detention and torture of peaceful demonstrators in Lhasa between September 1987 and March 1989, the outcome of events in Beijing might have been different. Asia Watch is currently compiling a report, to be published separately, that will provide data on recent abuses in Tibet. Here are a few of the matters that will be covered.

Six nuns, who demonstrated for Tibetan independence on Barkhor Street in Lhasa in October 1989 in front of martial law troops were seized "with the swiftness of a thunderbolt" by the Lhasa Public Security Bureau, according to a November 8, 1989 report in *The Guardian* (London). Nine others were detained after having interrupted a performance of a Tibetan opera in Norbulinka Park in Lhasa on September 2. Four Tibetan monks were sent without trial to labor camps for three years in early November for "shouting reactionary slogans" during a demonstration near Jokhang Temple, Tibet's holiest shrine, on October 25. Eleven other Tibetans, including ten monks, were sentenced at a mass rally in Lhasa on November 30 for the non-violent crimes of advocating Tibetan independence and printing "reactionary" leaflets. These cases are only a handful of some 50 cases of arrests or trials reported from Tibet since

September, and Asia Watch believes they are a fraction of the total.

Tibet may also have become a laboratory of torture techniques for the Chinese security forces. One of the men sentenced on November 30, Dhundup Dorje, 43, a driver at the Lhasa Shoe and Hat Factory, is believed to have been regularly beaten, resulting in partial deafness, and to have been chained hand and foot for three months in a cell he shared with 20 others. Nuns in custody appear to face a wide range of sexual abuse including rape and use of electric prods in the vagina. One horrific report dated March 2, 1989 and published in *The Guardian*[*] of a prisoner arrested after a one-hour demonstration in Lhasa in April 1988 says in part:

> Another two or three men touched my body all over with about 11 burning cigarettes, continuously for two hours. The Chinese used their belts so much that the metal buckle came off. They broke a chair over me. Then they had to stop for a rest because they were so tired.
>
> After that dogs bit me on the feet. Blood came out and my clothes were all ripped...

The account conforms to other accounts documented most recently in a November 1989 report by Physicians for Human Rights entitled "The Suppression of a People: Accounts of Torture and Imprisonment in Tibet."

The tactic which emerged in Beijing and other cities following the June 4 crackdown of encouraging, persuading or forcing people to inform on one another was already in effect in Tibet even before martial law was declared in Lhasa. In many cases, the torture seems to have been inflicted as a way of getting more names of protestors from those in custody.

A few days before the first anniversary of martial law in Lhasa, machine-gun posts were set up on roof-tops around the Barkhor Square and four tanks were moved into place outside the Jokhang Temple.[**]

The anniversary reportedly passed by without major incident.

---

[*]   November 8, 1989.

[**]   The Guardian (London), March 5, 1990; and Tibet Information Network Update (London), March 6, 1990.

8. THE BUSH ADMINISTRATION'S RESPONSE

The Bush Administration's policy towards China has been one of maintaining relations at any cost and explicitly sacrificing human rights in the process. The near-silence of the Reagan administration on human rights violations in China juxtaposed with its stridency on the Soviet Union showed a clear double standard. The Bush administration, however, has shown outright hypocrisy by coupling its public expressions of concern with behind-the-scenes efforts to patch things up with those responsible for the slaughter and arrests following the June 4 crackdown. The symbolism of a top-level US delegation meeting in secret on the Fourth of July with the Chinese leadership who crushed the democracy movement, and again on International Human Rights Day, December 10, will stand as the hallmark of the Bush Administration's human rights policy this year.

The Bush Administration's willingness to let the Chinese government set the terms of US-China relations became evident in February when President Bush visited Beijing. On February 26, he hosted a barbecue to which the American ambassador, Winston Lord, had invited Professor Fang Lizhi, China's most outspoken dissident and human rights activist. Embassy officials told the press that the invitation was meant to signal concern about human rights.

But that concern was not shared by the White House which made it known before the event that the President would probably not meet with Professor Fang. In any case, there was no opportunity: uniformed Chinese police physically prevented Fang from attending the dinner.

In final meetings with Chinese leaders before his departure, the President expressed only "regret" over the incident. The White House then went out of its way to say that the invitation to Fang had not been the President's idea and blamed the US embassy for the fiasco. The message could not have been clearer: President Bush was more concerned with soothing the sensibilities of the Chinese authorities than with defending human rights.

Quite apart from his studied avoidance of China's most famous advocate of basic freedoms, the President also ignored "talking points" on human rights prepared for him by his staff for use at the dinner. Throughout January and February, intellectuals in China, inspired by Professor Fang, had sent petitions to Deng Xiaoping and the National People's Congress urging that political prisoners such as Wei Jingsheng, imprisoned since 1979 for writing an article urging that China's modernization program include democracy, be amnestied. Their hopes that the US President would give a boost to their efforts were dashed.

In March, martial law was declared in Tibet following a demonstration on March 5-7 in which Chinese troops followed Politburo member Qiao Shi's exhortation to be "merciless." Dozens were killed, more than 300 arrested. The State Department made a public statement deploring the violence and excessive use of force against demonstrators, but it did not mention China by name and did not express its views directly to the Chinese leadership - undoubtedly to avoid offense.

From mid-April onward as student demonstrations in Beijing and elsewhere gathered strength, avoiding offense appeared to become a guiding principle of the Bush administration. The President and Secretary of State studiously avoided any comment on the growing democracy movement, and at no time did they publicly suggest that there would be serious repercussions if the authorities responded violently. Lower level officials were only marginally more forthcoming.

The Administration refrained from public comment when martial law was declared on May 20. Administration sources have said President Bush made private demarches to Deng Xiaoping, urging him not to use force against the students, but it is not clear how forcefully that message was conveyed.

After the tanks rolled in to Tiananmen Square, the administration wasted precious hours "watching and waiting" before condemning the random massacre of civilians. Secretary Baker, appearing on Cable News Network just after massive violations had been extensively reported, said that, "it would appear that there may be some violence being used here on both sides." He declined to discuss whether the Bush Administration would consider sanctions against the Chinese, stating that "Before we get into hypothetical situations, let's see how this most recent and extremely deplorable development unfolds...." It was already abundantly clear what would unfold, and Baker's refusal to hypothesize was a refusal to condemn human rights violations.

On June 6, after considerable prodding by the Congress, the Administration reluctantly imposed limited sanctions on China, including a suspension of sales of military items, suspension of visits between US and Chinese military leaders, and a "sympathetic review" of requests of Chinese students for asylum. But it was clear even as he announced the sanctions, that President Bush was unenthusiastic about applying economic pressure on China. [*]

At a news conference, the President stated that "I don't want to hurt the Chinese people. I happen to believe that commercial contacts have led, in essence, to this quest for more freedom." The President went on to state that "I think that it's important to keep saying to those elements in the Chinese military, 'Restraint. Continue to show the restraint that many of you have shown.'" [**] The ferocity of the army's action against the demonstrators and the subsequent round-up of democracy movement participants can hardly be called "restraint."

Not content with the Bush Administration's tepid response, the US Congress responded almost immediately to the crackdown. Within days, dozens of sanctions bills had been introduced by both Republicans and Democrats in the Congress. On June 20, the House Banking Subcommittee on International Development Institutions and Finance held a hearing to discuss the United States position on loans to China in the multilateral development banks. [***] The Administration refused to send a witness to the hearing, but faced with the near certainty of the Congress taking legislative action to force it to vote against

---

[*]   The President's fears about "hurting people" was rather disingenuous — no such concern was expressed when the US imposed sanctions against Nicaragua, Cuba, or Vietnam.

[**]   The Washington Post, June 6, 1989.

[***]   By law (Section 701 of the International Financial Institutions Act) the United States representatives to the multilateral development banks are required to vote against loans to governments engaged in a pattern of gross violations of internationally recognized human rights.

China, it announced later that day that it would seek to postpone new multi-lateral development bank loans to China. It also suspended "participation in all high-level exchanges of Government officials" with the People's Republic of China.[*]

The sanctions announced by President Bush on June 6 and the subsequent decision to oppose loans to China in the banks was as far as the Administration was willing to go, despite calls in Congress for more extensive measures, such as a suspension of China's Most Favored Nation trade status and an end to high technology exports. Though the President promised to review other aspects of the US-China relationship, there appears to have been no consideration of additional sanctions, notwithstanding the country's deteriorating human rights situation. Moreover, at no time did the Administration state clearly what the United States expected from the Chinese if sanctions were to be lifted. Worse, the Administration began undercutting the few sanctions it did impose almost immediately.

On July 9, the Administration announced its decision to sell three Boeing jetliners to China, valued at $150 million. (A fourth aircraft was delivered in August.) The delivery had been halted, along with all other military sales, in June. The items are considered "dual-use" because their navigational equipment can be used for military purposes. The change in policy was justified by White House Chief of Staff John Sununu, who stated that "There was some indication a few days ago by the leaders in China that they were going to try to extend the hand [of conciliation] back to the students....That was a constructive step."[**] No such "constructive step" took place; in fact, the repression got worse.

In October, the ban on military sales was further weakened when the 42 Chinese military officers assigned to work on Project Peace Pearl, a $500 million program to upgrade Chinese fighter aircraft, were permitted to resume their work. The officials had been taken off the project at the time of the President's

---

[*]   The New York Times, December 19, 1989.

[**]   The Washington Post, July 10, 1989.

announced sanctions. On December 20, President Bush waived a Congressional ban on the export of three communications satellites to China.[*] Secretary Baker justified the sale - which should have been prohibited under the President's own sanctions package - as being in the United States "national interest."

According to press reports, the only arms deal with China which now remains on hold is the shipment of an $8.2 million contract for submarine torpedoes and torpedo launchers.[**]

The Administration also undermined other aspects of the sanctions package. Immediately following the events of June 3-4, the Export-Import Bank (a US corporation which provides loans to US businesses seeking to invest overseas) quietly stopped processing Chinese loan applications. The State Department held up the applications for two weeks, then began processing loan applications as if nothing had happened. In November Congress accepted an amendment by Senator Helms on the International Finance Act which barred Export-Import Bank financing to China, subject to a presidential waiver on the grounds of "national interest." The President signed the bill into law on December 19 and immediately waived the China provision. *The New York Times* reported on February 6, 1990 that Export-Import Bank resumed its lending with a $9.75 million loan to China National Offshore Oil Corp.

The Bush Administration attempted to export its own tepid response to China to its Asian allies. On July 6, Secretary Baker met with foreign ministers of the Association of Southeast Asian Nations (ASEAN) and urged them not to adopt additional sanctions against China. When meeting with the Japanese Prime Minister, Baker apparently warned Japan not to "isolate" China. This effort to lobby other countries against forceful measures to protest the killings and arrests sent another signal to the Chinese that the US was not concerned about human rights.

Despite the alleged ban on meetings between Chinese and US officials, Secretary Baker met with the Chinese Minister in July during an international conference on Cambodia. In September, representatives from the US Trade Representative's office held meetings with Chinese officials to discuss China's

---

[*]   The ban had been imposed at the initiative of Senator Albert Gore (D-TN).

[**]   The Washington Post, December 12, 1989.

entrance into the General Agreement on Tariffs and Trade (GATT) — a move ardently sought by the Chinese government. Although in conversations with Human Rights Watch, USTR officials stated that they conveyed their opposition to China's admittance to the GATT in conversations with the visiting officials, they also admitted that as a result of the widely publicized meeting, Chinese entrance was brought a step closer.

By October, administration officials were quietly testing Congressional waters about the feasibility of resuming support for China in the multilateral development banks. House and Senate leaders, however, made clear their opposition to such a move.

On November 21, the House of Representatives passed a bill containing sanctions against China. The measure was passed in the Senate on January 30, 1990, and signed into law. The legislation included a ban on Overseas Private Investment Corporation (OPIC) insurance for U.S. investment in China, a suspension of export licenses for the sale of munitions, crime control equipment, and sattelites, and a prohibition on the liberalization of COCOM controls on the sale of high technology goods. (The bill also included "sense of Congress" language advising the President to suspend Export-Import Bank financing and to vote against loans to China in the World Bank.) The Bush Administration had strongly objected to sanctions legislation and, in negotiations with House and Senate conferees on the bill, National Security Advisor Brent Scowcroft threatened that the President would veto the bill unless it included a presidential waiver which significantly weakened the measure.

Symbolically, the most important action by the Bush Administration of the year was its decision to send a high-level delegation, including National Security Advisor Brent Scowcroft and Deputy Secretary of State Lawrence Eagleburger to China on December 9. (Ironically, President Reagan had sent Eagleburger to Poland in July 1983 under similar circumstances but with a very different message: that the US would lift some sanctions imposed after martial law only if Poland released all its political prisoners.)

Anticipating the outrage which greeted the news of the Scowcroft-Eagleburger mission, the Administration's decision was made in absolute secrecy. Congress was not consulted, and, it appears, even the State Department's Asia Bureau seemed unaware of the plan. The enduring symbol of the Bush Administration's human rights policy towards China will be the televised image of General Scowcroft, drink in hand, toasting the Chinese leadership with these words: "We extend our hand in friendship and hope you will do the same." He then went on to say in a callous slap at those Chinese now in prison for their advocacy of peaceful change, "In both our societies there are voices of those who seek to redirect or frustrate our cooperation. We both must take bold measures to overcome these negative forces."[*]

The symbolic significance of the December visit cannot be overstated. The posture of the US delegation was clearly meant to placate Beijing and apologize for the rupture in ties imposed by Washington after Tiananmen Square, despite the fact that the Chinese did not make a single move toward curbing human rights abuses.

Faced with a barrage of criticism, President Bush did further damage, justifying his decision by stating that he is looking for ways to find "common ground" with Beijing, and noted that "We have contacts with countries that have egregious records on human rights."[**] Secretary Baker attempted to justify the mission by stating that human rights were on the agenda, and noted that China's leaders "[are] going to have to help us" if good relations between China and the US were to be restored.[***] President Bush made it abundantly plain that the West should not expect any reciprocity in the near future from the Chinese for the United States' extraordinary gesture, stating that "time is required" before Beijing's full response can be evaluated.[****]

There would be yet one more revelation in 1989 which eclipsed even the December mission. On December 18, the White House revealed that National Security Advisor Scowcroft had made a secret trip to China in July, just weeks after the crushing of the democracy movement. The trip had been kept secret and was only revealed when it was reported by Cable News Network. (The Secretary of State apparently deliberately misled the Congress about the July visit when he said that the December trip was the first high level visit by the US.)

The Administration stated that the purpose of the July mission was "to show the sense of purpose and direction of the US Government." But it clearly

---

[*]   The Washington Post, December 10, 1989.

[**]   The Washington Post, December 12, 1989.

[***]   The Washington Post, December 11, 1989.

[****]   The Washington Post, December 17, 1989.

violated the President's June 20 statement, suspending all high-level exchanges with China.

In November, the Administration opposed an important Congressional initiative which would have granted safe haven to Chinese students with J-1 visas in the US. On November 30, the President announced that it would veto legislation to permit Chinese students to stay in the United States, and, instead, said that he would grant the students a four-year extension in the US through administrative fiat.* Because the actual benefits to Chinese in the US under the President's action are at least arguably more generous than the Congressional measure, it can only be assumed that the President vetoed the legislation to avoid offending the Chinese by disassociating himself from the hugely popular Congressional measure. The President's success on January 25, 1990, in sustaining his veto by obtaining 37 votes for it in the US Senate - four more than the one third of the Senate he needed - was greeted by his Administration as an endorsement, or a mandate, for the Administration's China policy.

The Chinese were offended anyway. An official response published by *Xinhua News Agency* (and issued on the very day of Brent Scowcroft's arrival in Beijing) said the decision to implement the extension of stays by administrative means "grossly interferes in China's internal affairs, runs counter to Sino-US agreements on education exchanges and hurts Sino-US relations. China's State Education Commission hereby expresses its great indignation and strong protest against it."

The Bush Administration also exhibited a singular lack of generosity towards Chinese nationals who fled their country after the June 4 crackdown. A group of more than 100 student leaders, dissident writers, intellectuals and independent trade unionists escaped to Hong Kong following the crackdown. France, alone among the Western democracies, speedily accommodated the asylum requests of about 70 of them. The rest remained in limbo, fearing detention and possible repatriation if they revealed their whereabouts to the authorities. Instead of making it known that the Chinese would be welcome, the US threw up bureaucratic obstacles and admitted only a handful.

Perhaps the one salutary response made by the Administration after the Tiananmen Square bloodbath was the welcome decision to offer sanctuary to

---

* The president did not technically veto the bill. Since Congress had adjourned, presidential inaction on the bill would normally have constituted a "pocket veto." Instead, President Bush sent a memorandum of disapproval to the Congress indicating that he was returning the bill to the legislative branch.

Fang Lizhi and his wife, Li Shuxian, at the US Embassy in Beijing on June 6. Unfortunately, similar concern was not demonstrated about the fate of dozens of other activists. Ren Wanding, a human rights activist imprisoned during the Democracy Wall movement and prominent among the demonstrators in Tiananmen Square, went to the US Embassy after the June 3-4 crackdown. Instead of being treated like a person in imminent danger and in need of assistance, he was read bureaucratic regulations and eventually left. He was arrested shortly thereafter and remains in detention.

By the beginning of January, President Bush seemed to be fishing for examples of positive measures which he could cite as evidence that the Chinese authorities were reciprocating his efforts to mend relations. In his news conference on January 5, the President cited China's granting permission to a Voice of America reporter to return to Beijing and its reiteration of a pledge not to sell missiles to the Middle East as a manifestation of progress. Letting a VOA reporter in is not the same as releasing prisoners and the promises on missiles have almost certainly been broken already.

On January 11, the Chinese government announced the lifting of martial law and the administration immediately took credit, with Vice-President Quayle calling it a "dividend" of the Scowcroft-Eagleburger missions. Without even querying whether the lifting of martial law would have any effect on the ongoing repression in China, the administration immediately announced its support for World Bank lending for loans for humanitarian assistance such as earthquake relief.

The administration's eagerness to let the Chinese off the hook must be contrasted again with the Reagan position on Poland. When Poland announced the lifting of martial law in July 1983, it also announced a limited amnesty, almost certainly in response to message from the Reagan administration that some sanctions would be lifted if political prisoners were released. But it then promulgated a package of new laws that left the most repressive aspects of martial law intact. The Chinese have done the same. But where the Bush administration rushed to welcome the end to martial law in China, the Reagan administration was far more cautious. "We're going to go by deeds, not words," said President Reagan and refused to lift the sanctions which were far more stringent than those imposed on China. The most important sanction of all as far as Poland was concerned — a veto on Poland's application to join the International Monetary Fund — was not lifted until all Solidarity prisoners were released.

The contrast with the Bush administration's refusal to publicly acknowledge the thousands in prison in China could not be more obvious.

9. CONCLUSION

When asked how they view the West and its people, ordinary Chinese often reply: "In the West, we're told, human feelings are as thin as paper." This negative image of the West is one that has been assiduously propagated by the government-controlled media in China over several decades as a means of bolstering and validating official claims of the "superiority of socialism," and to fend off the allegedly "corrupting" influence of Western-style "bourgeois liberalism." For the countless Chinese citizens who either participated in or supported last summer's pro-democracy movement in Beijing and other cities of China, the Bush Administration's unseemly haste in moving to restore normal relations with the present Chinese regime, a mere seven months after the massacre by Chinese government troops of somewhere near a thousand unarmed civilians in Beijing, can only have served to reinforce this impression of superficiality and inconstancy on the part of the West.

The contrasts and ironies of the time are manifest. In an inverse proof of the "domino theory," Eastern Europe has all of a sudden moved in the direction of the open society, showing the enormous resources of peaceful popular uprisings against a type of social system whose outward display of strength and immovability merely served — and in China's case still serves — to conceal a profound brittleness. Violent repression by Eastern Bloc leaders was always a possibility during the recent uprisings, and the so-called "Tiananmen solution" was reportedly under active consideration by East Germany's former ruler, Erich Honecker, at the time of his ouster. But in the event only in Romania, the most repressive of the Eastern Bloc states, did the depth of antagonism between rulers and ruled lead to an attempted, indeed expanded, replay of the Tiananmen scenario, bringing massive violent confrontation and widespread killings before the ending of tyranny could be achieved. China's leadership, which only last November sent an official communique to Ceausescu expressing its desire for still closer links with "socialist Romania, that wonderful country,"* was thrown into consternation by the fall of its one remaining ally in Eastern Europe, and responded by drastically stepping up security measures in Beijing.** At the same time, we saw the Bush Administration all but encouraging the Soviet military to intervene on the side of the Romanian people in order to ensure their victory over tyranny.

The Administration however — cleaving to a flawed and outmoded strategic analysis which holds the maintenance of close ties with China to be the key to any successful containment of Soviet expansionism — has reverted since June 4 to a shabby double standard insofar as the question of human rights in China is concerned. Ever since Deng Xiaoping's return to power in 1978 and throughout the subsequent decade of reform in China, successive US administrations have allowed the geopolitical assessment to submerge any concern that they may have felt at the well-documented continuance of serious human rights abuses in Deng's China, starting with the suppression of the Democracy Wall movement in 1979 (many of whose leading figures, such as Wei Jingsheng, still languish in Chinese prisons today). As a result of this *realpolitik* approach by the US and other leading Western nations, China's leadership has come to feel that it can violate the human rights of its citizens with virtual impunity, with no major cost to its international diplomatic and business relations. Witness the comment made by Deng Xiaoping some years ago: "When we imprisoned Wei Jingsheng, the West did nothing."***

From various statements made by Chinese leaders after the Tiananmen crackdown last June, it is clear that they were genuinely surprised at even the very limited condemnatory measures subsequently adopted by the West. Indeed, had the West only been more vocal and insistent in its advocacy of the cause of human rights in China during Deng Xiaoping's decade of reforms, it

---

*   AFP, December 23, 1989; in FBIS, December 26.

**   See for example, Washington Post, December 26, 1989.

***   Quoted in the CPC Central Committee's Document No.1, January 1987.

is conceivable that the Chinese leadership, weighing the likely costs and consequences of its actions, might have pulled back from the brink and refrained from ordering the bloody military assault on Tiananmen Square last June. Instead of a major tragedy, significant progress towards democracy in China such as that recently seen in Eastern Europe could well have ensued. And in view of Deng Xiaoping's reported recent characterization of Mikhail Gorbachev as being the chief culprit responsible for the collapse of communism in Eastern Europe (a "dirty flood of revolts"),[*] it is surely time that the US proponents of old-style 'China card' diplomacy began to reassess their former assumption that a greater geopolitical interest requires the curtailment of US expressions of concern about human rights in China.

The argument given by President Bush against the adoption by the US Administration of firm and resolute measures to condemn the gross violations of human rights committed by the Chinese regime on and since June 4, 1989, has consistently been that he does not want "to isolate the Chinese people." But why, apparently, did such commendable scruples and anxieties not arise in the course of the Administration's wholeheartedly enthusiastic response to the recent epochal events in Eastern Europe? Had Nicolai Ceausescu's last-ditch resort to wholesale violence and bloodshed by the hated Securitate forces succeeded, rather than leading as it did to his own overthrow and execution, would the Romanian people too have been "isolated" by the inevitable Western reaction — the imposition of severe economic and diplomatic sanctions? The people of Beijing and of other Chinese cities last summer were no less determined in their demands for fundamental social and political change in China than were the people of Romania last month — and on the night of June 3-4, 1989 they were every bit as insurgent, fighting the tanks of the ironically-named People's Liberation Army with their bare hands. The crux of the matter, as regards President Bush's expressed desire not to isolate the Chinese people, is his clearly implied view that the interests of the Chinese people are best served by not upsetting or challenging the interests of the present Chinese leadership. But here again, if radical political change and the overthrow of entrenched elites is good for Eastern Europe, why is the main thrust of US policy now towards maintaining all possible links with those who ordered the massacre in Beijing and, at every opportunity, to draw a discreet veil over the brutal events of last

---

[*] Washington Post, January 8, 1990. See also New York Times, December 28, 1989.

summer?

Even when judged by its own standards, this *realpolitik* approach is both short-sighted and self-defeating. For the fact is that the post-June 4 regime in China is unquestionably more deeply unpopular, despised and hated by its citizens, particularly in the cities, than any since 1949 — and its days are clearly numbered. When Deng Xiaoping, Li Peng and Yang Shangkun ordered the troops into Beijing and authorized them to open fire on the peacefully insurgent citizenry, they crossed their Rubicon just as surely as Ceausescu crossed his when he ordered the massacring of innocents at Timisoara. The crucial difference (and perhaps the only salient one) between the uprisings in China and in Romania, was that in the latter case the army eventually sided with the people. There was, however, clear evidence in the former case of widespread disaffection among PLA soldiers and officers, and it is possible that the Chinese military, having examined the Romanian example, will react quite differently next time. Previously respected by the people, the PLA has suffered an enormous loss of popular prestige as a result of the crackdown, and it must be aware that there is only one clear way to restore its credentials.[*]

In weighing how to respond to the tragic events in China, it should be firmly borne in mind that the main political casualty of the post-June 4 repression in China has been the very sizeable constituency of reform-minded intellectuals, policy-makers and senior Party and government officials that was previously moving steadily towards a commanding position. This constituency extends throughout the country, is particularly strong in the coastal provinces and in the capital, and it undoubtedly represents the main hope for future democratic reform and economic renewal in China. The cautious indifference of the West towards the failure of the popular democratic movement in China, and its increasing eagerness to return to business as usual with an outwardly triumphant

---

[*]	According to the South China Morning Post of December 28, 1989, Yang Baibing, Chief Political Commissar of the PLA, revealed in an unpublished speech made in early December that: "The commander of the Beijing-based 38th Group Army and another 110 officers and 1,400 soldiers refused to take orders or left their posts during the People's Liberation Army crackdown on the pro-democracy movement in April and June." Continued the Post: "According to Mr Yang, 21 officers and cadres with ranks of divisional commander or above, 36 officers with ranks of regimental or battalion commander, and 54 officers with the rank of company chief 'breached discipline in a serious manner during the struggle to crush the counterrevolutionary rebellion' in June. In addition, 1400 soldiers 'shed their weapons and ran away.'" Finally: "Mr Xu Qinxian, head of the Beijing-based 38th Group Army...was reportedly court-martialled in the autumn and given a stiff sentence." And according to the Far Eastern Economic Review of January 4, 1990: "One well-placed [Western intelligence] analyst estimates that the number of PLA personnel court-martialled or executed around June 4 1989 was 'in the low hundreds.'"

but internally beleaguered regime, only serves to delay the eventual return to power of this reformist camp and to diminish its current ability to resist and assert itself.

For the present Chinese leadership, there can be no going back — any resumption of democratization or of real political reform is manifestly out of the question, for it was these very processes which brought the regime into confrontation with its own people in the first place, in a crisis to which the regime knew and offered only one answer: bloody repression. Wholesale intimidation and tight authoritarian control are the only instruments by which the present Chinese regime can maintain its position of power over society, and it cannot afford to relax these except in superficial ways useful for external purposes. Amid the nauseatingly self-congratulatory rhetoric accompanying the lifting of martial law ("The martial law has fulfilled its historic mission... It added a shining chapter to the history of the republic"),[*] the regime is even now preparing for the next round of violent confrontation with its citizens.

An article in the *Liberation Army Daily* on December 2, 1989, for example, described in considerable detail the various items of repressive equipment that China's "mobile forces" urgently need to obtain, including: "A certain number of high-speed vehicles for pursuit and patrolling purposes...and some special vehicles with large engines that are collision resistant and bulletproof so that they can be used to remove all roadblocks and intercept armed thugs." In addition: "Other vehicles should be improved in their technical properties so that their tires cannot be punctured, their doors and windows cannot be smashed and their bodies cannot be approached or burned." Plans for computerized anti-riot command centers, "in the [PLA's] headquarters and in all general brigades," were said to be already at the implementation stage.[**]

The Chinese, perhaps more than any other nation, look to history for answers, and in this case they do not have to look very far. In April 1976, three months after the death of Premier Zhou Enlai, hundreds of thousands of Chinese gathered in Tiananmen Square to express their grief and to protest the recent rise to power of the ultra-leftist "Gang of Four," Mao's closest allies. The

---

[*]   People's Daily, January 11, 1990.

[**]   FBIS, December 28, 1989. Moreover, according to the Wall Street Journal, January 2, 1990: "At the highest level, China has created a group under the Communist Party's Central Committee to deal with potential disturbances, according to Chinese sources. The Urgent Contingency Preparatory Group is headed by 85-year-old Deng Xiaoping."

security forces and the People's Militia were promptly unleashed on the crowds, and hundreds were injured before the Square was finally cleared of demonstrators and "returned to the people." This first "Tiananmen Incident" was at the time declared by the authorities to have been a "serious counter-revolutionary disturbance," and a period of deep repression followed throughout China. The population was cowed, and it soon retreated into sullen acquiescence; but it never forgave the regime for the bloodshed in the Square.

In September 1976 Mao Zedong died — his political reputation and popular esteem in tatters — and within days the more progressive elements of the Chinese leadership had staged a peaceful coup. The "Gang of Four" was placed under military arrest, activists imprisoned after the April demonstrations in the Square were released and rehabilitated, and the Tiananmen Incident itself was soon declared by the new regime to have been, after all, a "wholly revolutionary action" on the part of the people of Beijing. Deng Xiaoping's time had come at last, and the reforms soon began.

The scale and size of last summer's popular protests in China against official corruption and lack of democracy simply dwarfed that of the 1976 protests in Tiananmen Square. Then, the military was not used, nor has it ever been proven that a single person died in the course of that crackdown; but the regime of the "Gang of Four" was nonetheless doomed by its actions then. Several hundred and perhaps as many as a thousand Chinese citizens, the overwhelming majority of whom were unarmed peaceful demonstrators or just plain onlookers, were slaughtered on the streets of Beijing last June. The Chinese people — who doubtless recall well that even at the height of the civil war between Communists and Nationalists in late 1948, the KMT military commander of Beijing chose to surrender peacefully to the People's Liberation Army rather than allow fighting and bloodshed among Chinese to take place in the capital — will sooner or later exact retribution from those who ordered this act. Deng Xiaoping, once a hero to his people, has now destroyed his own reputation just as Mao did.

Having prevailed thus far in its battles with Congress over China policy, the Bush Administration has a responsibility to alter its course radically, if it is not to inspire universal cynicism over its claims to espouse human rights. Yet the very fact that the Administration has scored a political victory such as the January 25 vote in the Senate that fell short of overriding the President's veto of legislation on the Chinese students in the US makes it unlikely that such an alteration of course will take place. Accordingly, the burden of trying to shape

74

a policy that reflects concern for human rights still rests largely on the Congress.

The choice before the US Congress, as it debates how best to respond to the Administration's shamefully supine policy in recent months towards the unrepentant tyrants of Beijing and their ongoing suppression of the pro-democracy movement, should be decided by one consideration above all others. Namely, does the US want to signal to the Chinese people, and to the reform-minded majority of its intellectual and governmental elite who will inevitably return to power some day soon, its resolute commitment to the cause of democratization and freedom in the communist world? Or will it, by default and inaction, rest content to convey the message that the US people and its govern-ment are but fair-weather friends of that cause, so betraying the hopes of countless numbers of Chinese citizens who last summer looked to the West, and the US in particular, as a source of inspiration? If so, the impressions of America that will stick in China are, firstly, of how its television camera crews were always there in the Square to record the scenes of exultation and triumph before June 4, and to take home the sound-bites for prime time audiences; and secondly, of how once the ensuing bloodshed had begun and the movement's crushing defeat had been thoroughly recorded, the camera crews — and with them the interest and concern of the US government — simply packed up and went elsewhere.

APPENDIX

ARRESTS IN CHINA SINCE JUNE 4, 1989

March 8, 1990

NB: This list is updated and additional biographical details are added as information becomes available. The number of those arrested is reported by official sources to be over 6000 and may be as high as 30,000. **This list is cumulative and supersedes that of January 30, 1990.** An alphabetical index of all names appears at the end, and asterisks distinguish between individuals sharing the same name.

1. INTRODUCTION

Repression in China continues, with at least 40 officially confirmed death sentences and executions and a continuing extensive purge of individuals associated with last year's pro-democracy movement. The latest reported death sentences, on a worker and an unemployed person, were imposed in Beijing in early December 1989. Three more persons, convicted of participating in the Chengdu riots of early June, were executed on November 7. And on October 14, a man was executed in Jinan, Shandong Province, after being convicted of having burned a vehicle on June 6. For the most part, however, the official media has curtailed its earlier open reporting of arrests and executions, almost certainly in response to international criticisms of the purge. Moreover, the majority of those detained or arrested since June 4 have been held incommunicado, often in secret locations.

Many of those arrested have been accused of non-violent acts, *e.g.* "spreading rumors," or "distributing counter-revolutionary handbills." While many others have been accused of acts of vandalism, arson or other crimes, there is no way of judging from the official media reports what the basis for such charges is. Chinese radio and television reports have singled out for particular attention those cases in which individuals have allegedly engaged in violence or have had previous convictions. However, the majority of those detained appear to be being held by the authorities solely on account of their involvement in peaceful protests.

On July 8, Chinese authorities listed five crimes that would henceforth carry punishments ranging from "reform through labor" to death, including "propagating and actively supporting the spread of bourgeois liberalization." This suggests that the non-violent advocacy of political reform could now be viewed as a capital offense in China.

The vast majority of those brought to trial and sentenced since June 4 for their pro-democracy activities have been either workers or unemployed. In a significant new development, however, the authorities have recently begun to conduct secret trials of students. Six Beijing students, all from the College of Foreign Affairs, a prestigious institute for the training of future diplomats, went on trial in November, according to *Reuters* (December 11, 1989). Four were convicted of "counterrevolutionary crimes" and two were convicted of theft; the court imposed sentences ranging from seven to ten years' imprisonment. Sources, requesting anonymity, told *Reuters* that the trials had been closed even to families of the accused. The names of the students are not yet known.

Those executed thus far were tried in what can only be termed summary proceedings, although the trials and appeals were in accordance with a 1983 decision of the National People's Congress to speed up adjudication of internal security cases. By the terms of that decision, which has the force of law, the defendants have only three days to appeal. There has been no mention in the press of any defense counsel. Also, there is no tradition in China that the defendant is presumed innocent, although legal reformers have been pressing for adoption of this principle since the enactment of a Criminal Procedure Code in 1979. Instead, "confessions" extracted by force or intimidation are common; it appeared that several of the prisoners who made public recantations on television in the past months had been subjected to severe physical abuse. In addition to those sentenced to death, many prisoners recently arrested have been sentenced to "reform through labor" in equally summary trials, or else have been sent for "re-education through labor" — a form of detention without trial. In both of the latter cases, the prisoners are likely to end up in the Chinese gulag, a vast network of labor camps, where conditions are reported to be extremely harsh. If the experience of prisoners arrested after the Democracy Wall Movement of 1978-79 is any indication, detained leaders of the independent student and worker federations face years of solitary confinement and hard labor.

To prevent any further escapes of individuals now being sought for their involvement in the democracy movement, the Chinese government sealed the country's borders and changed its visa regulations. All exit permits issued before June 20 are now invalid, and holders of current passports are required to get new permits at the Public Security Bureau (PSB, the equivalent of the police). Anyone obtaining a foreign visa now has to go back to the PSB for a second permit. In addition to changing these regulations, security has been tight at China's airports and train stations, and there have been numerous arrests of people in the departure area of Beijing's international airport, and instances of people having been dragged off planes.

Individual cases of some of those reportedly arrested or executed are outlined below. It should be noted, however, that the great majority of detentions or arrests carried out in China since June 4, 1989, have not been publicly announced by the authorities, so no details are available.

2. DEATH SENTENCES AND EXECUTIONS

MENG Duo, 24, an unemployed worker, and ZHOU Jiguo, a restaurant employee, were tried and sentenced to death in early December, 1989, by a Beijing court on charges of murdering a policeman on June 4, 1989 according to a recent report in *Beijing Wanbao* (in *Associated Press*, December 8, 1989). A third co-defendant, CHEN Yong, a worker from Tangshan, was sentenced to life imprisonment. The three allegedly attacked and killed LI Guorui, 20, a member of the People's Armed Police, at 5:00 a.m. on June 4 as government troops were converging on Tiananmen Square. According to *Beijing Ribao*, the sentences reflected the government's determination "to strike severe blows against the criminal activities of counterrevolutionary elements and to protect the security of the state." The report gave no indication as to whether the executions had been carried out; but since Li Guorui has been officially declared a "martyr," reprieves for Meng and Zhou are extremely unlikely to be granted.

The Sichuan Provincial Radio Service (in *FBIS*, November 9, 1989) reported the names of three men sentenced to death on November 7 by the Chengdu City Intermediate People's Court. ZHOU Qi, HE Xiaokang and CHEN Guangping were found guilty of "unbridled beating, smashing, looting and burning" during the June 4-6 riots in Chengdu. They allegedly attacked the police, engaged in robbery, set fire to a movie theatre and destroyed shops (according to Chengdu Radio, cited in a BBC broadcast of November 7). Three others, WU Baiming, LI Ying and YANG Jin were executed on charges of murder and theft apparently (but not certainly) unrelated to the June pro-democracy events. All six appeals before the Sichuan Provincial High People's Court were rejected, according to Amnesty International (ASA 17/98/89, November 16, 1989). A public sentencing rally preceded the executions. Chengdu was the scene of a major conflict between police and demonstrators in June, in which as many as several dozen people were killed by the security forces.

SUN Baohe was executed in Jinan, Shandong Province, on October 14, according to *Reuters* (October 20, 1989). The *Jinan Masses Daily* of October 15 reported that Sun, together with two others, had been convicted of burning a *Shanghai*-brand vehicle on June 6. Sun was sentenced to death, while his co-defendants — WANG Lixin, a factory worker, and WANG Yong, an office worker — each received 10-year prison terms.

YU Chunting and GUO Zhenghua were executed on July 29 after being sentenced to death by the Wuhan Intermediate People's Court. They were charged with murdering two civilians, stabbing a soldier and stealing his gun during the pro-democracy unrest in May in Wuhan, according to July 31, 1989 dispatches from *Reuters* and *UPI*. The execution report appeared in the *Guangming Daily*, which did not give precise details of the murders. YU was said to have served a sentence in a labor camp and GUO was described as a criminal. DENG Wenbin, allegedly an accomplice, was sentenced to death but given a two-year reprieve. Two others were sentenced to life imprisonment and nine more were convicted on charges of assaulting police, damaging railway property, and inciting people to attack Communist Party and government offices.

Two peasants, LI Wenbao, 20, and LIANG Hongchen, 18, accused of stealing bicycles and money, were sentenced to death on July 26, 1989 by the Beijing Intermediate People's Court after being convicted of "indulging in violence" following the military crackdown of the democracy movement on June 4, 1989. They had three days to appeal their sentences. LI is from Shunyi County, a suburb of Beijing, and LIANG is from a suburb of Shenyang.

WANG Guiyang and ZHOU Xiangcheng, peasants from Sichuan Province, were sentenced to death on July 1, 1989 in a public trial by the Chengdu Intermediate People's Court. They were convicted on arson charges for having burned vehicles in Chengdu on June 5. Their appeals were turned down by the Sichuan High People's Court, and the two were executed by firing squad on July 8. A third man, HE Qiang (Jiang) was sentenced to death but given a two year reprieve.

Seven people were executed in Beijing on June 21, 1989: LIN Zhaorong, CHEN Jing, ZHU Jianjun, WANG Hanwu, LUO Hongjun, ZHANG Wenkui and BAN Huijie. An eighth person, WANG Lianxi, a woman, was apparently spared. All eight had been sentenced to death by the Beijing Intermediate People's Court on June 17. Their appeals to the Beijing Supreme People's Court were turned down.

Lin Zhaorong had been a worker at Huimin Hospital in Beijing and had served a previous sentence of three years' forced labor for "hooliganism," according to a Beijing radio broadcast. He was accused of setting fire to a military vehicle on June 5. Luo Hongjun was a ticket-seller for the Beijing

Municipal Public Transportation Company; he was accused of looting supplies from military trucks. Ban Huije, a peasant from Xinle County, Hebei, was a contract laborer in Beijing; he was accused of beating up soldiers, and of knocking one of them unconscious.

Seventeen executions were carried out in Jinan on June 20 after the condemned prisoners were paraded through the streets. The *Jinan Daily*, a local newspaper, reported that the 17 were among a group of 45 people sentenced to death or imprisonment after an open trial. Beijing radio said the trial was attended by 10,000 people. Nine prisoners were given a two-year deferral of their sentence during which they will have to do forced labor, but the others were given deferred sentences, according to a *UPI* report.*

XU Guoming, a brewery worker; **BIAN Hanwu,** unemployed; and **YAN Xuerong,** a radio factory worker were publicly executed on June 21 in Shanghai after an afternoon session of the Shanghai Intermediate People's Court upheld their death sentences. They had been sentenced to death by the Shanghai court for setting fire to a train that had plowed through a group of demonstrators on June 6, killing six and injuring six others. The demonstrators had been blocking the track to protest the massacre in Beijing. The men were arrested, together with eight others: **PENG Jiamin, WEI Yinchun, YANG Xiao, SUN Jihong, AI Qilong, YUAN Zhimin, ZHAO Zhimin** and **ZHU Qin.** All were accused of having "smashed railway cars, setting fire to nine railway cars and six public security motorcycles, turning over police boxes and beating up firemen to impede them from putting the fire out," according to a Beijing newspaper account. According to Wang Shuquan, deputy chief procurator, all pleaded guilty, except for ZHU Qin. Shanghai radio announced that ZHU would be released "after education." It is not clear how the Shanghai People's Sub-procuracy, which charged the men, singled them out from the other demonstrators. Warrants of arrest were issued on June 8, and the first three were tried under Article 110 of China's criminal code. Xu, Bian and Yan had

---

* The evidence that the 17 executed in Jinan on June 21 were connected with the pro-democracy demonstrations is as follows. The UPI report states: "An undetermined number of anti-government demonstrators were among 17 people put to death in the northeastern city of Jinan Wednesday for various crimes, the Jinan Daily reported." In addition, Tokyo NHK reported on June 22 that 17 executions had been carried out on June 21. The report added that Beijing Radio had reported on June 21: "[T]he Intermediate People's Court in Jinan...held trials opened to the masses and handed down death penalties, life imprisonment and penal servitude for definite terms respectively on 45 political offenders who caused great damage to public peace and order. Hence it is believed that the executed are 17 among those 45." (In FBIS, June 22, our emphasis.)

three days to appeal.

LIU Baode, a "hooligan," was executed by shooting after his sentencing on November 30 by the Municipal Intermediate People's Court in Beijing. In an unprecedented move, the sentence was announced in the official press without details as to the time and place of arrest or the alleged crimes (*Beijing Ribao*, December 1, 1989; in *FBIS*, December 20, 1989). At the same time, **SU Peng,** a "hooligan", was sentenced to death (*Beijing Ribao*, December 1, 1989; in *FBIS* December 20, 1989). His sentence was suspended for two years and he was deprived of his political rights for life. Neither Liu's nor Su's connection to the pro-democracy movement is known, but the way in which their sentences were reported gives strong reason to suspect that they were in fact pro-democracy activists. (See above, p. 22.)

3. ARRESTS OF HONG KONG AND MACAO CHINESE

On December 25, 1989 the *China News Agency* (Zhong Xin She) announced that three Hong Kong Chinese — **LUO Haixing, LI Peicheng** and **LI Longqing** — and two Chinese from Macao — **XIE Zhenrong** and **CHEN Zewei** — had been formally placed under arrest by the public security authorities of Guangdong Province for their alleged involvement in the "underground railroad", a Hong Kong-based network which has secretly helped over 100 pro-democracy activists to escape from China since June 4.

According to the report, Luo Haixing was arrested on October 14 by border guards at Shenzhen while attempting to help top democracy-movement leaders Wang Juntao, Chen Ziming and others escape to Hong Kong. Luo Haixing is the son of Luo Fu, a former editor of the Hong Kong *Xin Wan Bao* (New Evening News). The *China News Agency* report accused Luo Haixing of having "conspired" since July this year with Cen Jianxun, a leading member of the Hong Kong Alliance in Support of the Patriotic Democratic Movement in China (the main umbrella organization for pro-democracy groups in Hong Kong), to operate the "underground escape channel." The report also accused the Hong Kong Alliance of being "dedicated to the overthrow of the Central People's Government and to the incitement of domestic turmoil" in China.

Luo's case is being handled not by the Guangzhou Public Security Bureau, but by a special group sent to Guangzhou directly by the Ministry of State Security and charged with looking for "pro-democrats on the run" (*Ming Bao*, December 22, 1989; in *FBIS*, December 22, 1989). The arrest notice from the Public Security Bureau prohibits family visits and noted that Luo, 40, might be sentenced in two to three months time. A visit request from his father, former editor-in-chief of the Hong Kong *Xin Wan Bao*, was refused by the Ministry of State Security. Luo, a representative of the Hong Kong Trade Development Council in Beijing from 1986 until March 1989, when he began to operate his own import-export business, was last seen by his brother on October 16, 1989; his whereabouts were unknown until his family received notice of his arrest in mid-December. Luo holds a Hong Kong British passport. According to *Reuters* (December 21, 1989) the British Embassy has made inquiries, but the Chinese authorities have refused to comment. They regard Luo as being a Chinese national.

In 1983, Luo's father, Luo Chengxun (Luo Fu), was sentenced by a Beijing Municipal Court to 10 years imprisonment for spying for the U.S., but was quickly released. He now resides in Beijing.

Li Peicheng, a resident of Hong Kong, entered China on October 12 and was arrested in Zhanjiang, Guangdong Province on the following day, according to the report. He had allegedly "used addresses, names and liason codes supplied to him by the Hong Kong Alliance" in an attempt to smuggle Chen Ziming and the others, then in hiding in Zhanjiang, out of China.

Li Longqing, also a resident of Hong Kong, was arrested on December 5 in Shenzhen, according to the *China News Agency* report; it stated that Li had worked together with Li Peicheng during the failed October mission to rescue Chen Ziming, Wang Juntao and others, but it made no mention of how he had evaded capture at that time.

The report also states that two Macao residents, Xie Zhenrong and Chen Zewei have been formally placed under arrest by the Guangzhou public security bureau for their alleged role in trying to assist the Beijing student leader **Zheng Xuguang** to escape. Chen, 29, a Chinese major and vice-chairman of the Macao student union, was one of three students from Macao, taken into custody on July 27 by a special team sent to Guangzhou from the national office of the Public Security Bureau. All three were students at Jinan University in Guangzhou. From their homes in Macao where they were on leave, they traveled to Guangzhou on July 26 without informing their families. On August 11, the families received an anonymous phone call that the three had been detained. This was later confirmed by the Macao office of *Xinhua News Agency*.

The two other students, **QIN Guodong** (Chun Kwo-tung), 21, a medical student, and **LIANG Xihua** (Leung Sai-wai or Shehua), 23, a student of international finance, were released on August 23 after having been detained for almost a month. They have returned to Macao. A fourth student, Hong Kong resident **TSE Chun-wing**, about whom little is known, was still in custody as of August 24. He, too, was accused of helping activists in the democracy movement escape through Guangzhou.

4. ARRESTS OF CHINESE STUDENTS AND INTELLECTUALS

Two intellectuals who headed the Chinese authorities' recently released "most wanted" notice, **WANG Juntao** and **CHEN Ziming**, together with Chen's wife, **WANG Zhihong**, were arrested near Canton while following a secret escape route in a bid to reach Hong Kong, according to Asia Watch sources and *Reuters* (November 9, 1989). **FEI Yuan**, an editor on the now-banned journal *Economic Studies Weekly*, may also have been arrested. Several people from Hong Kong and Macao, who had entered China to escort the group to safety, were arrested at the same time. The total number of those caught in the police swoop, which is thought to have been based on a tip-off provided by someone within the exiled pro-democracy movement, could be as high as 20.

Wang Juntao (alias Wang Xiaojun) and Chen Ziming (alias Li Bin) have played a key role in China's unofficial movement for democracy ever since 1976, when both were arrested and jailed in the wake of the April 5 "Tiananmen Incident." At that time, popular mass demonstrations in Tiananmen Square against the regime of the "Gang of Four" were violently suppressed by the authorities; two years later, however, the Tiananmen Incident was officially reappraised as having been "entirely revolutionary in character." During the "Democracy Wall" movement of 1978-80, Wang, a native of Henan, founded and edited an unofficial pro-democracy magazine called *Spring of Beijing*. He was by then an alternate member of the central committee of the Communist Youth League. In 1980, as a physics student at Beijing University, Wang stood as an independent candidate for election to the Beijing local legislature, in the first openly-contested elections ever to be held in the PRC. Prior to the crackdown, Wang, 31, was a leading member of the Beijing Institute of Social and Economic Sciences, the associate chief editor of *Economic Studies Weekly* and deputy director of the Beijing Young Economists Association.

Chen Ziming, 37, is from Haiyan County in Zhejiang. Until June 4, he was director of the Beijing Institute of Social and Economic Sciences, a pioneering private research organization. The specific role played by Chen and Wang Juntao in the recent pro-democracy movement in Beijing is still unclear, but it is thought that both were active as behind-the-scenes strategists and as advisers to the protesting students.

The two topped a Ministry of Public Security list, issued in June, of China's seven most-wanted intellectuals, but they had managed to evade arrest until the authorities' release in October of a new "wanted" list. Also named on this list are: Wang Zhihong (see above), 32, from Shanghai; **WU Xuecan,** 38, from Binhai County in Jiangsu, an editor and journalist on the *People's Daily Overseas Edition*; **LIANG Qingtun** (alias Liang Zhao'er), 20, from Pengxi County in Sichuan, a student at the Psychology Department of Beijing Normal College; **CHAI Ling,** 23, from Rizhao City in Shandong, a postgraduate student at the Child Psychology Research Institute of Beijing Normal College; and her husband **FENG Congde,** 22, from Sichuan Province, a postgraduate student at Beijing's Remote Sensing Institute. (Chai and Feng were both top leaders of the Tiananmen Square protest movement.) According to *Ming Bao* of November 3, the wanted notice accuses the seven of being "important criminals who incited, organized and directed the Beijing counterrevolutionary riot. They have committed serious crimes and have run away out of fear."

Asia Watch has received confirmation that the famous writer and journalist **WANG Ruowang** has been arrested. He is believed held incommunicado in No. 1 Detention Center in Shanghai. According to Asia Watch's latest information, Wang went into hiding after June 4, 1989 but later returned to Shanghai to face his accusers, and was then, in mid-September, placed under arrest. His wife, **YANG Zi,** has apparently not been arrested, although she may be under house arrest. Further confirmation of Wang's arrest was given in an *AFP* report of October 31, which quoted a Party official who requested anonymity as having said: "Wang Ruowang was arrested more than a month ago on orders from Beijing." The official added: "We don't know the fate of the people arrested. Even their families don't know where they are and have to go to the police station to deliver mail and tend to affairs."

On October 20, two articles sharply criticizing Wang Ruowang appeared in Shanghai's *Wen Hui Bao* and *Jiefang Ribao* (Liberation Daily). His activities during the pro-democracy movement were listed as follows: listening to the Voice of America and spreading rumors based on its broadcasts; writing articles in support of the student hunger-strike and giving "counterrevolutionary" speeches on Shanghai's People's Square; and publishing articles in the Hong Kong press. He also participated in a demonstration march in May in support of the student movement. It was stressed that Wang would have to be severely punished for such activities. He was also castigated in the Shanghai press for having said of the movement: "I am very happy. It is a wonderful sight. The long-awaited day has finally arrived."

Wang, 71, was a member of the Communist Party from 1937 until early 1987, when, in the wake of the large-scale student demonstrations of the preceding winter, he was expelled from the Party along with dissident intellectuals Fang Lizhi and Liu Binyan.

An Asia Watch source has reported the arrests of a group of *Renmin Ribao* journalists. **WU Xuecan**, 40, an editor named on an October "wanted" list; **SONG Yuchuan**, 39, who holds a Master's degree in law; reporters **HOU Jie**, 20, and **JIN Naiyi**, 30; and **FAN Jianping**, an editor, are all reportedly in custody. In addition, **LI Jian**, from *Wenyi Bao*, a Beijing weekly, has also been detained. No other details as to the circumstances of their arrests are available.

ZHAO Yu, a member of the Shanxi Province Writer's Association and author of the sports exposé "Qiang Guo Meng" (Dream of a Strong Country), who disappeared shortly after June 4, 1990 is now known to have been arrested in Shanxi. The date of his arrest is, however, still unclear (*Shijie Ribao*, February 12, 1990). Shao, a signer of the May 16 Declaration, encouraged other writers to participate in the demonstrations at Tiananmen Square; he was also commander-in-chief of the intellectual contingent there. Zhao, whose trial is pending, was reportedly freed on bail before the Chinese New Year.

A number of prominent Shanghai intellectuals and students — **CHEN Lebo, RUAN Jianyun, CHEN Qiwei, YU Zhongmin, SHI Binhai, YANG Lujun, WANG Youcai** and **ZHAO Wenli** — were reportedly arrested during the summer and autumn of 1989. All were cited as "agitators" in "The Facts about the Shanghai Riot," a June 28, 1989 article in the Shanghai daily, *Wen Hui Bao*. The article was later reprinted in other major Chinese newspapers.

CHEN Lebo and **RUAN Jianyun** are both journalists. Chen, now in his forties, was director of the domestic economic section of the Shanghai newspaper, *Shijie Jingji Daobao* (World Economic Herald); Ruan was deputy director of the newspaper's Beijing office. Chen was charged with joining the pro-democracy movement and engaging in "counter-revolutionary propaganda," according to *Shijie Ribao* (World Journal, October 19, 1989). The arrests of Chen and Ruan have been independently confirmed by an Asia Watch source, although the arrest dates are not known.

CHEN Qiwei, 33, a vice-director of the Economics Department at East China Normal University, was reportedly arrested in August. He had written articles and given lectures during the pro-democracy period, promoting the idea that political reform should precede economic change.

Chen Qiwei, Chen Lebo and Ruan Jianyun are all believed to be held incommunicado at No.1 Detention Center in Shanghai.

YANG Lujun, a researcher at the Asian Institute of the Shanghai Academy of Social Sciences, was arrested in August. He is said to have been actively involved in the democracy movement and to have visited Hong Kong in May.

YU Zhongmin and SHI Binhai were reporters for *Fazhi Yuekan* (Law Monthly, published in Shanghai by the East China Institute of Government and Law), and were also arrested for their involvement in the democracy movement, according to *Shijie Ribao* (October 10, 1989). The arrest dates are not known.

Two others mentioned in "Facts about the Shanghai Riot," WANG Youcai and ZHAO Wenli, are believed arrested although the arrests have not been confirmed. Wang, general secretary of the Beijing Students Autonomous Federation, attempted to organize continued student resistance in Shanghai after the June 3-4 crackdown in Beijing, according to *Renmin Ribao* (People's Daily, September 24, 1989). Zhao Wenli, a female student from the class of 1988 at Northwestern College of Politics and Law, was identified in the article as the former head of the Student Propaganda Delegation to the South. She was said to have gone to universities in Shanghai on May 24 to "stir up problems."

On December 7, 1989, LIU Jianan, 38, was sentenced to ten years imprisonment and deprived of his political rights for two years by the Changsha Intermediate People's Court (in *FBIS*, December 14, 1989). According to the official *Hunan Ribao*, Liu is said to have listened to "the enemy radio" of Taiwan from May 1989 on, and to have tried to maintain contact with the station. Liu, a former teacher at Changsha's 25th Middle School, is also accused of sending 16 counterrevolutionary letters from Changsha, Yueyang and Wuhan to KMT secret agents, and of "organizing, publishing and distributing reactionary books."

SONG Min, a history major at Beijing Normal College and a graduate of the Institute of Aviation, was arrested together with a Hunan classmate in Xiangxi, Hunan Province. Song went into hiding around May 20, 1989; the date of his arrest is not known.

According to the Hong Kong newspaper *Sing Tao Wan Pao* quoting from dissident sources in Hong Kong, Chinese authorities have arrested eight Lanzhou (Gansu Province) University student activists for their part in the pro-democracy movement (*Agence France Presse*, in FBIS January 8, 1990). Three of the arrested were reportedly on the official list of most wanted student leaders. Asia Watch cannot independently confirm the report, but it is known that Lanzhou University sent a delegation, reportedly including 800 students, to Beijing during the pro-democracy protests. On January 11, an official at the university said she knew nothing about the previous report and denied there was a new wanted list; no new lists, she said, have been published in local newspapers since June 1989. Unofficial Chinese sources reported, however, that regional governments have issued their own lists apart from the Beijing ones; such lists are not made public but secretly circulated in security units. (*FBIS*, January 11, 1990.)

Hong Kong's *Ming Bao* (January 24, 1990, in FBIS, January 29, 1990) refuting earlier reports, asserted that **WEN Yuankai**, prominent lecturer and biophysicist at China University of Science and Technology in Hefei, Anhui Province, has not been arrested. According to the report, Wen, 43, is still at the university and is engaged in a "self-review." However, he is neither giving lectures nor is he "free in his movements" and must obtain permission before leaving the campus. He has been expelled from the Chinese Communist Party for "adhering to the stand of bourgeois liberalization and openly declaring opposition to the four cardinal principles." The China University of Science and Technology was the birthplace of the student protest movement of winter 1986-87; at that time Fang Lizhi, China's leading dissident figure and a close friend of Wen Yuankai, was the university's vice-chancellor.

TIAN Qing, distinguished music historian and Deputy Director of the Institute of Music in the Chinese Academy of Arts, Beijing, was arrested on September 23, 1989 according to an Asia Watch source. He is believed to be held incommunicado in the Erlong Detention Center in western Beijing. Tian, a Tianjin native in his early forties, had been under investigation since his denunciation for giving a lecture on June 4 at the Shanghai Music Conservatory describing events he had witnessed in Beijing on June 3.

ZHENG Di, a journalist on the magazine *Jingjixue Zhoubao* (Economics Weekly), has been arrested while trying to flee the country, according to an Asia Watch source.

CHEN Bo, from Beijing University; **LIU Xiaofeng,** deputy director of the Structural Reform Institute, and nine others (names unknown) from the Institute; **WU Jiayang** of the Chinese Communist Party Central Office; and **WANG**

Xiaoping, an editor at the Workers' Publishing House have all been arrested, according to an Asia Watch source. Dates and places of arrest are unknown.

WANG Hong, a second year English student at Zhejiang Teachers University in Jinhua was arrested on campus when he returned from summer recess, probably in early September. He is reportedly being held incommunicado, denied visits by his family. Wang, in his early twenties, is charged with burning posters bearing quotations from Mao and with using his own blood to write slogans.

OUYANG Ping, a lecturer at the Institute of Sociology at Beijing University, was taken into custody at the same time as two other Beijing intellectuals, **SUN Li** and **LU Liling,** previously reported arrested by Amnesty International (ASA 17/66/89). Sun was a graduate of the Institute of Sociology at Beijing University; LU, 35, was a member of the editorial department of the journal *Development and Reform* of the Research Institute for the Reform of the Economic Structure. Amnesty also reported the arrest of a fourth intellectual, **ZHOU Yongping,** another teacher at Beijing University's Sociology Research Institute. No additional details are available.

MA Ziyi, 38, a lecturer in the history department at East China Normal University, is believed to have been arrested shortly after the student leader, Wang Dan, was captured on July 2, 1989. Wang is said to have used Ma's apartment as shelter for a short period prior to his arrest.

CHENG Kai, chief editor of the *Hainan Ribao* and a Zhao Ziyang supporter, was arrested on July 19, 1989, according to *Tuanjie Bao* (Solidarity News, September 5, 1989) and *Huaqiao Ribao* (Overseas Chinese Daily, July 19, 1989). This arrest has not been independently confirmed.

ZHANG Cunyong, 27, an instructor in the department of management, Beijing Institute of Steel, was arrested on June 15, together with his sister (name unknown) and **HOU Xiangjun.** Zhang was active in the democracy movement prior to the June 4 crackdown; afterwards he edited and printed information about the repression. His sister and Hou are said to have assisted in the printing.

According to *Beijing Wanbao* (June 7, 1989) **HU Jinping,** a member of the Autonomous Federation of University Students from Outside Beijing, was arrested for setting fire to military vehicles on June 6.

LI Xiaolu, XIA Ming and **YANG Jun,** all students at Beijing Normal University, are reported to have tried to hide a submachine gun on June 6. According to a report in *Beijing Ribao* (July 7, 1989), they were turned in by informers after June 20.

ZHENG Mingxia, treasurer of the Beijing Students Autonomous Federation is reported to have been arrested on July 27, 1989.

DUAN Xiaoguang, a Nanjing University professor of philosophy in his early 30's, was reportedly arrested in Shenzhen around August 30, 1989 while attempting to leave for Hong Kong.

CAI Sheng, a grade 2 student at Wuchang Senior Middle School, was handed over to the police by Harbin Engineering University on June 8, 1989. He is accused of having lied that his sister was a student at the Politics and Law Department of Beijing University and was killed on campus by a shot to the chest, and of stealing a mini-cassette and other articles while housed overnight by sympathetic students at a Harbin university. According to a report in the June 7 *Heilongjiang Ribao* (in *FBIS*, August 4, 1989), Cai asked for leave on June 3 and took a train to Harbin. He later confessed that he went there to develop some film and do some shopping, but after seeing some leaflets he decided to "take advantage of the opportunity to cheat." On June 6, he allegedly made a speech in front of Harbin Construction Engineering College, saying he was a senior middle school student from Jilin and was an eyewitness to the events of June 4 in Beijing, where he saw many students killed in Tiananmen Square by vehicles running over them. He also said he lost his watch and 300 yuan at the Square.

WANG Jianxin, deputy director of the Historical Preservation and Museum Science section of Northwest University in Xi'an, was arrested on campus sometime during the first half of September, according to an Asia Watch source. Wang had written an independent wallposter account of the serious clash between police and student demonstrators which occurred in Xi'an on April 22, in which he blamed the police for the violence. He also wrote letters to Deng Xiaoping, Li Peng, Zhao Ziyang and the Supreme People's Court and Procuracy calling for a government investigation into the causes of the "April 22 Massacre" in Xi'an, and he helped organize a protest demonstration there on May 17. Wang has been held incommunicado since his arrest.

SU Ding, 32, Dean of the East-West Art Institute of the Sichuan Academy of Social Sciences, has been formally charged by the Sichuan Provincial Government with political crimes allegedly committed in late May or early June. According to an Asia Watch source, Su made speeches, participated in demonstrations and attended meetings, all of which were branded "anti-Party."

Su was arrested in late August in Beijing while buying an international air ticket. He had been invited to serve as a Visiting Scholar this year at Arizona State University, and his travel documents were all in order. Su, a specialist in aesthetics and literary theory, was forced by the Sichuan Party authorities to write a series of "self-criticisms" this past spring after he had recommended for publication a book which was later denounced as being "anti-Party." He is thought to have acquired the taint of "bourgeois liberalism" through this and other similar acts. Su is believed held incommunicado.

The arrest of **XUN Jiansheng**, 34, an instructor in Marxist philosophy at the Sichuan Provincial Youth League College, was announced at a mass rally in Chongqing on September 13. According to the following day's *Chongqing Evening News*, Xun spoke out in his classroom, on June 8, against the government repression in Beijing; for this offence he is charged with "counterrevolutionary propaganda and incitement." According to the October 10 Hong Kong paper *Ming Bao*, Xun Jiansheng was denounced to the authorities by one of his pupils, who reported Xun to have said, "Several hundreds or even thousands of people were killed in Beijing." Xun has reportedly been expelled from the Party and dismissed from his post, and is now being held in a detention centre in Chonqqing. His family have not been informed of his whereabouts; they learned of his arrest and of his appearance at the mass rally only from a television report.

The same article in *Ming Bao* also mentioned the recent arrest and sentencing to two and three years "re-education through labour" of six unnamed persons, mostly workers, apparently in connection with the pro-democracy movement in Chongqing.

YUE Wenfu, a student at the Lu Xun Academy of Literature and a leading activist in the Tiananmen Square occupation, has been arrested and badly beaten while in prison, according to an Asia Watch source. Yue is thought to have helped erect barricades in Beijing in order to block the PLA's entry into the capital.

SHAO Jiang, 22, a member of the central committee of the Autonomous Students Union of Beijing Universities, was arrested on September 1, 1989 near the border between Zhuhai and Macao, according to the Hongkong *China News Agency* report on September 3. Four others were arrested at the same time. Shao had been a mathematics major at Beijing University and was deputy secretary-general of the Beijing University Self-Rule Preparatory Committee.

LI Jinjin, about 30, was arrested on June 12 at his home in Wuhan. He was a doctoral student in constitutional law at Beijing University. He also worked as an instructor at the Institute of Law and Politics in Beijing. Up until the time of the student demonstrations in April and May, Li had been head of the official Graduate Students Union at Beijing University. He was arrested at gunpoint, according to an Asia Watch source. From Wuhan he was transferred to a detention facility in Beijing. Family members have been permitted to drop off clothes for him but as of late August, they had not been allowed to see him.

WU Xiaoyong, the producer of an unauthorized radio program which announced on June 4 that thousands had been killed in the military crackdown, was arrested at the end of August, according to *Asiaweek*. Wu is the son of the former Foreign Minister, Wu Xueqian.

SONG Lin, a professor of Chinese Literature at East China Normal University in Shanghai is reported to have been arrested in early September. Song led a march of students and workers on June 9 in Shanghai to protest the killings in Beijing; the demonstrators put up barricades to block traffic. Interviewed under a pseudonym several days later, he said, "Some people think the time for peaceful action is over and we should go on to acts of sabotage. But I think the better attitude is one of passive non-cooperation." Song had been warned in mid-June that he was on a wanted list.

CHANG Jin, a treasurer of Beijing University's Independent Student Union, is reported to have been arrested. Neither the date and place nor the circumstances of his arrest are known. Chang was a geography student at Beijing University.

ZHANG Ming, 24, from Jilin City, Jilin, a student at Qinghua University's Department of Automobile Engineering, was arrested in Shenzhen in September, according to a report in the Hongkong newspaper *Ming Bao* (September 14, 1989). The article quotes "sources in Shenzhen," but Asia Watch has not been able to confirm the report independently. Zhang Ming was on the "21 Most Wanted" list issued by Chinese authorities in June.

YANG Lang, vice-director of the reporters' section of *Zhongguo Qingnian Ribao*, has reportedly been arrested (*Zheng Ming*, October 1989). Yang is alleged to have led the United Association of Capital (Beijing) Intellectuals and to have been a key organizer in rallying support for the student movement.

HU Ji, a history professor at North-West University and author of two books on Shaanxi history was arrested on September 16, 1989, according to a report in the Hong Kong newspaper *Ming Bao*. Hu was said to have given speeches in

Xin Cheng Square in Xibei supporting the students. There is no official confirmation of his arrest.

ZHANG Cai, a student in the College of Management of Fudan University, Shanghai, was arrested on June 11 by the Public Security Bureau, "while trying to flee Shanghai under the escort of the third secretary of a certain foreign consulate," according to a lengthy article in Shanghai's *Jiefang Ribao* of September 7, 1989. He has apparently given lengthy "confessions" which form the basis of the newspaper article, detailing the activities of the Self-Government Union of College Students (SGUCS). [NB: An Asia Watch source reports that "Zhang Cai" may be an alternative name used by Yao Yongzhan, the well-known student detainee whose case is detailed below, p. 121.] Several other students and teachers are mentioned as having taken active roles in the demonstrations organized by SGUCS but it is not clear whether they have also been detained. Their names are **YE Maoqiang,** a young faculty member; and **GU Gang** and **LI Guangdou,** graduate students in journalism at Fudan University.

Several students and intellectuals, including two known to be detained (Liu Xiaobo and Zhou Duo: see index), are quoted in a *Xinhua* article of September 18, 1989, entitled "Witnesses Report No Deaths at Tiananmen Square." The article says it interviewed one of the witnesses, singer Hou Dejian, at his home. No location is given for the other interviews and the context suggests the individuals may either have been interviewed in prison or the quotations were taken from "confessions." Those quoted include **GAO Xin,** one of the last hunger strikers; **SONG Song,** a surgeon of the Beijing Union Medical College Hospital; **SHAN Gangzhi,** a urologist on duty in Tiananmen Square; **ZOU Ming,** Engineering and Physics Department, Qinghua University; **DAI Donghai,** student in the Department of Thermo-energy, Qinghua University; **LIU Wei,** Chemical Engineering Department, Qinghua University; **ZHAO Ming,** member of the preparatory committee of the autonomous student union at Qinghua University and student of the Department of Engineering and Physics.

GAO, a political activist arrested in June for his leading role in the pro-democracy movement, was released around December 20, 1989 (*Reuters*, January 9, 1990). A former lecturer at Beijing Normal University, Gao reportedly received "very bad treatment" during the six months he was detained in a prison near Beijing. According to a *Reuters* source, "He was made to confess his mistakes and express the Communist Party's opinions about what the protests represented and what happened in June." In support of student demands, Gao and three others began a new strike on June 2.

LONG Xiangping, a teacher of English in the foreign languages department of Xiangtan University, Hunan, was arrested on June 19, 1989. She allegedly became involved in the pro-democracy movement at the university after the June 4 crackdown. Long, age 35-36, married and with one child about four or five-years-old, had participated in student protests and tried to organize strikes in factories and made a public speech. As of November 1989, Long still had not been formally charged. (Amnesty International, Urgent Action 34/90, January 24, 1990)

Asia Watch sources report the arrest recently of LI Nanyou, an editor at the World Knowledge Publishing House in Beijing; LIU Di, former editor of the unofficial journal *Beijing Spring*, which appeared during the 1978-81 Democracy Wall movement; LU Jiamin, an official in the All-China Federation of Trade Unions; and JIN Yan, an employee at the Children's Film Studio, who was arrested in Canton after the government had secretly videotaped her making a one-hour public speech protesting the June 4 massacre.

According to an Asia Watch source, CHEN Dali, an instructor in the history department at Chengdu University and a leader during the student demonstrations in Chengdu, was arrested after the June 5-6 conflict and killings by the authorities there. No additional details are available.

Seven people were tried in Kunming, Yunnan on September 16, 1989 on charges of having fomented a counter-revolutionary plot, according to the September 28 edition of the *Yunnan Daily*. It named the leader of the group as SHI Ying, 27, and said that on June 9, Shi had gone to the town of Zhuzhou in Hunan Province where he gave a public speech at the train station, denouncing the military assault in Beijing. He then went to Kunming "to take part in agitation," according to the report. He and three other co-defendants, SHANG Jingzhong, YU Anmin, and JI Kunxing, decided to found a "counter-revolutionary party"; they then established an underground magazine called *Pioneers*, circulated anti-government leaflets and put up counter-revolutionary posters, according to the article (in *FBIS*, October 5, 1989).

ZHENG Xuguang, 19, a student at the Beijing Aeronautics Academy and a native of Mi district in Hunan Province, was arrested, probably around August 11, 1989 in Guangzhou (Canton). ZHENG, one of China's "21 Most Wanted" student leaders, was reportedly attempting to leave the country.

LI Hongyu, a psychology student at Beijing Normal University, was taken

99

into custody in Chengdu, Sichuan, on July 30. A *Reuters* report said that police officers uncovered 216,000 yuan or $58,000 that had been donated to the Autonomous Union of Beijing Universities. The cash was said to have been hidden at her boyfriend's home. It had reportedly been given to Li Hongyu by one of the students on China's "21 Most Wanted" list, **LIANG Qingtun,** another psychology student. His fate is unclear. LI Hongyu was taken to Beijing from Chengdu on August 6 for investigation, according to the *Reuters* dispatch.

LIN Shengli, ZHANG Wei and **LIU Feng,** all students from Henan Province, were arrested August 11, 1989 by the Zhengzhou City People's Procurate, according to a Henan radio broadcast on August 22 (in *FBIS,* August 23, 1989).

Lin, 21, was a law student at Zhengzhou University and one of the founders of both the Zhengzhou City College Students Autonomous Federation and the Zhengzhou University Autonomous Federation, according to the broadcast. Both organizations have been declared illegal. The radio report said Lin organized a "massive" demonstration in Zhengzhou on May 22 and the next day was in charge of squads of students which stopped trains at a city railroad station. He then, according to the report, set up a radio station called the Voice of Democracy at Zhengzhou University. On June 4, he led students to factories around Zhengzhou, delivering "counter-revolutionary speeches" and urging workers to strike. He was detained on June 13 (though not formally arrested until two months later) while distributing "reactionary leaflets" at the Xinan County Hotel.

Zhang Wei, 22, was a freshman in the journalism department of Zhengzhou University. On June 5, the day after the crackdown in Beijing, according to the radio report, he gave "inflammatory speeches" at Erxi Pagoda in Zhengzhou together with a law student named "Yang X." The following day, Zhang set up a temporary radio station and broadcast reports such as "What Really Happened in Beijing" and news from the Voice of America. This "Voice of Truth" station continued for three days. Then on June 9, he and "Yang X" put up posters throughout Zhengzhou University campus "slandering principal party and state leaders." Zhang was detained on June 22; it is not clear what happened to Yang X.

Zhang Wei and Lin Shengli have been charged with counter-revolutionary propaganda and "inflammatory delusion."

Liu Feng, 19, was a second-year student in public health at Henan University of Medicine. A native of Jiaozuo City, he was accused of organizing demonstrations and taking a leadership position in the Zhengzhou College Students Autonomous Federation. The radio report said he led hundreds of students in Zhengzhou to travel by bus to Tiananmen Square and helped organize the Henan students there. Back in Zhengzhou on June 6, he organized more than 300 students in a seige of the University of Medicine's administration building, the radio report said. In the course of the siege, the assistant to the president of the college was wounded in the head. Liu was charged with counter-revolutionary propaganda, "inflammatory delusion," and disturbing public order.

LI Dejun, 25, was arrested in late July in Benxi County, Liaoning Province on charges of "counter-revolutionary instigation," according to a report in *Liaoning Ribao* (July 20, 1989). Li, a teacher at Canhekou Peasants' Middle School in Benxi County, reportedly sent letters to 13 different colleges and universities and on May 18, put up a big-character poster at the Caohekou railroad station saying, "Support the petition of college student hunger strikers." The report said he incited workers and peasants to work with the students to establish a multi-party system in China. It also said he "energetically advocated bourgeois liberalization, lavished praise on Fang Lizhi and others, and viciously attacked party leadership."

XIANG Dayong, a Beijing University student, was arrested for organizing a July 23, 1989 demonstration on campus, according to Amnesty International. The demonstration was attended by more than 300 students to mourn those killed as a result of the June 4 crackdown.

Three students, **CHEN Liangru, CHEN Yonghong** and **WANG Guangxin** were sentenced for "armed robbery" by the Miyun County Court, Beijing (*Beijing Wan Bao,* July 20, 1989). All three joined the democracy movement in May and were arrested on May 25. Chen Liangru was sentenced to ten years; the other two received eight-year sentences.

MA Lianggang, described in an Anhui provincial radio broadcast on July 29, 1989 as a "key member of the Hefei Independent Students Union" was arrested in Haikou, Hainan. The date of his arrest is not clear. (in *FBIS,* July 31, 1989)

LI Cuiping, secretary-general of the Beijing Autonomous Union of College Students from Other Regions and Provinces, was arrested in Baoding in Hebei, south of Beijing, according to the July 12 edition of *Hebei Ribao.*

TAO Yongyi, director of the propaganda department for the Beijing

Autonomous Union of College Students, was arrested in Mengcun Hui Nationality Autonomous County. The date of his arrest, also reported in *Hebei Ribao*, is not clear.

LIU Jinliang, CUI Guoxin, JIANG Zhu and **WANG Shuangqing** surrendered to public security bureaus in Nanpi, Huanghua, Luanping and Hengshui respectively (all in Hebei Province), according to *Hebei Ribao* (July 11, 1989). All had been involved in "illegal organizations" either in Hebei or in Beijing, according to the newspaper.

CHEN Peisi, a noted comedian, was arrested around July 25, 1989 for involvement in the democracy movement (*Press Freedom Herald* No.5, July 27, 1989).

QIN Weidong, arrested sometime before July 6, was a leader of a student autonomous union organized by Beijing Medical University, according to a report in *Hebei Ribao* (July 12, 1989).

Amnesty International in its document ASA 17/64/89 has reported the arrests of several members of the Sichuan Academy of Social Sciences in Chengdu including **WANG Zhilin**, 35, a researcher and editor; **DU Qiusheng**, 38, and **LI Jing**, 33, researchers in the Institute of Philosophy and Culture; and **LI Xiaofeng** and **WANG Chengzhong**, researchers.

XU Chong, general secretary of an independent students' union in Anhui Province, was arrested in a hotel in Nanjing, the provincial capital of Jiangsu, according to the July 22, 1989 *Xinhua Daily*. He was among 3,782 people arrested in the three-day period July 13-15 in Jiangsu, according to that report.

Public security officials who made the arrests reportedly uncovered $1000 which, according to the same report, had been hidden by **CHENG Mingxia**, a student leader, who was said to have been arrested earlier in Beijing.

LI Guiren, editor-in-chief of the state publishing house, Huayue, in Shaanxi Province was arrested for trying to organize a strike of publishing house employees, according to *Legal Weekly*, a journal published in Shaanxi. He called a meeting the day after the military crackdown in Beijing, urging workers to sign a protest declaration and go on strike. He was also accused of organizing four demonstrations during the month of May and of writing slogans calling for the removal of Li Peng and Deng Xiaoping. The date of his arrest is not clear.

YE Wenfu, a poet and army officer, was a signer of the May 16 declaration issued by the Beijing Union of Intellectuals which called on the government to accept student demands. The date of his arrest is not clear. The Hong Kong paper *Ming Bao* (July 20, 1989) reports that he has undergone torture and has tried to commit suicide but these reports are not confirmed.

YU Haocheng, director of the Legal Institute of the Capital Iron and Steel Institute and former director of the public security bureau-linked Mass Publishing House, was one of 12 intellectuals who made a public appeal to the government to declare the student movement a "patriotic democracy movement." He is reported in custody, but the date of his arrest is not clear. His name is included on a list of about 40 names drawn up by the Politburo of Zhao Ziyang supporters who were collectively termed the "Anti-Party Coalition," according to a report in the *South China Morning Post* of May 27, 1989.

ZHENG Yi, a writer in his 40's who signed the May 16 declaration noted above, is believed to have been arrested during the first week of July. A native of Taiyuan, Shanxi Province, he was reportedly preparing a report on the student movement and had collected voluminous materials which are believed to have been confiscated. He was a frequent contributor to *People's Literature* and *Literature Monthly* and was a board member of China's Writers' Union.

KE Yunlu, a writer and signer of the May 16 Declaration, previously reported in custody, is now known to have been arrested in Shanxi Province sometime after June 4, 1989 (*Shijie Ribao*, February 12, 1990). Released on bail prior to the Chinese New Year, he awaits trial.

BAO Tong, 56, a senior adviser to Party Secretary General Zhao Ziyang, was reportedly arrested several days prior to June 3. According to *Shijie Ribao* (February 20, 1990), Bao Tong is being held in solitary confinement in Qincheng Prison, on a severely inadequate diet. While other inmates of Qincheng are said to have been treated better recently, Bao Tong "remains the exception."

He had been head of the Communist Party's Political Reform Research Center since January 1988 and was a member of the Central Committee. He is identified with the reformist views of his mentor, Zhao Ziyang, but rejected Western-style democracy as "irrelevant" for China, according to an article in the *Asian Wall Street Journal* (December 26, 1988).

YANG Guansan, head of the Social Survey System at the Research Institute of State System Reform, an institute associated with Zhao Ziyang, is reported arrested, together with **GAO Shan,** deputy director of the Political Structual Reform Research Center of the Communist Party. GAO Shan, according to Beijing Mayor Chen Xitong's June 30 speech to the National People's Congress

Standing Committee, took part in a meeting on May 19 which called for an emergency meeting of that Committee in light of a decision of the Politburo to impose martial law. **WU Wei,** bureau chief of the same research center, is also reported to be in custody.

WANG Luxiang, a prominent signatory of the May 16 declaration and a co-producer of the controversial television series "River Elegy" (He Shang), who was arrested last June, has now been released, according to *Shijie Ribao* of February 25, 1990 (citing Hong Kong *Wen Hui Bao.*) "River Elegy" depicted China as being subject to periodic political upheavals like the ebb and flow of the Yellow River, and it highlighted the differences between the "transparency" of democracy and the "opacity" of autocracy. The series' main author, SU Xiaokang, is known to have escaped.

BAO Zunxin, another leading intellectual is believed to have been arrested shortly after issuance of the secret warants, according to Chinese sources. He was a magazine editor and associate research fellow at the Institute of Chinese History under the Chinese Academy of Social Sciences.

CAO Siyuan, a senior advisor to Party Secretary General Zhao Ziyang and the director of Stone Corporation's Institute for Social Development Research, was arrested on May 30. Cao had been active in calling for an emergency session of the National People's Congress to be convened, in order to overturn the imposition of martial law.

ZHOU Duo, 42, an economist with the Stone Corporation, China's largest computer firm, was arrested on July 10, according to Asia Watch sources. At the time of his arrest, he was head of two departments in Stone, the Strategic Planning and the Public Relations Departments. Prior to his joining Stone, he had been a lecturer in the Economics Department of Beijing University and before that, had taught at the cadre training institute of the Communist Youth League. Several senior staff of Stone have been either arrested or have fled into exile. The Institute for Social Development Research of the Stone Corporation is accused of having led a petition drive to call for an emergency meeting of the Standing Committee of the National People's Congress following the declaration of martial law on May 20, 1989. A letter of May 21 containing the names of 57 Committee members said that "the will of the people should be reflected through legal procedures." According to one account, the May 21 letter also called for the dismissal of Li Peng.

LI Jiangfeng, 21, a student at the Beijing Iron and Steel Institute, was arrested on June 15 in Hebei and accused of being a leading member of the Autonomous Federation of Beijing College Students. Taken into custody by the Qinhuangdao City public security bureau, he was accused of burning six military vehicles in Beijing. Hebei officials turned him over to the Beijing public security bureau. (See YANG Yijun, in index.)

LIU Fuan, a student in the department of basic science at Beijing Medical University, was also arrested in Hebei by the Zhangjiakou City public security bureau. The arrest took place some time in mid-June. He reportedly made a "confession," according to *Hebei Ribao* (June 17, 1989) but the specific charges against him are not clear. He is said to have been a leader of the student movement in Beijing.

DAI Qing, China's best-known woman journalist who wrote a regular column for *Guangming Ribao,* a Beijing daily popular among intellectuals, was arrested on July 14, 1989, her apartment ransacked, and manuscripts and articles confiscated, according to press reports from *UPI* and *Reuters.* Since her arrest, Dai has been ordered to write a detailed account of her activities in connection with the democracy movement. What she has written to date is said to have failed to please her interrogators.

Dai was originally reported held incommunicado in a maximum security prison near Beijing. However, she "recently" was permitted a visit to her ailing father-in-law in a Beijing hospital, sources close to the family reported (*South China Morning Post,* December 7, 1989). She was escorted to and from Qincheng prison by two guards and has not, as previously rumored, been released, paroled, or placed under house arrest. An appeal for her early release by the current Guangdong governor, who is the son of Dai's stepfather, the late Marshal Ye Jianying, was unsuccessful.

During the last week in January, Dai Qing was moved from Qincheng Prison and placed under house arrest in a Beijing suburb (FBIS, February 9, 1990). She is confined to a guesthouse, but may read books and periodicals and receive visits from her husband and daughter. Her family has been informed that investigation into her activities has been completed and that she will not be brought to trial.

Dai, in her early 40's, made her reputation publishing censored information, such as the story of the repression of Trotskyite cadres in the 1950's, and was involved in numerous literary publications. She helped rally other journalists to the support of a popular Shanghai editor, Qin Benli, when he was fired from his job at the *World Economic Herald* by the Shanghai party chief in April 1989. At one stage during the student demonstrations in Tiananmen Square, just prior to the visit of Soviet President Gorbachev, Dai went to the square to persuade students to leave because she feared a government crackdown.

Dai was named in Beijing Mayor Chen Xitong's June report listing intellectuals and activists considered by authorities to have engaged in serious antigovernment activity. She has been accused of slandering the government and belonging to an illegal organization. Activities for which she has been criticized include signing an appeal in the May 15 *Guangming Daily* asking the government to recognize the legality of the student movement, and her June 4 resignation from the Communist Party. In February 1989, Dai attended the banquet President Bush gave in Beijing.

YANG Wei, 33, a graduate student in biology at the University of Arizona, was arrested on July 18. He had returned to China in late 1986 from the United States and was arrested in January 1987 for his alleged role in student demonstrations which broke out in December. He was also accused of involvement in the U.S.-based organization, Chinese Alliance for Democracy, which publishes the journal *China Spring* and is believed to have funding from Taiwan. Sentenced to two years in prison, he was released in January 1989. His political rights had been suspended for a year, however, and he was unable to return to the United States to continue his studies. The government news agency reported on July 18 that he refused to "show penitence" after his release and continued to incite students to oppose the government.

ZHANG Shu, a reporter for the *People's Daily*, is also reported under arrest, although the date of his arrest is not clear. According to an Asia Watch source, he wrote a special edition of the paper after the executions of three workers in Shanghai (June 21, 1989) describing the Politburo meeting during which Communist Party Secretary Zhao Ziyang was removed from office.

The edition was photocopied and circulated, although it was never actually printed. Zhang and six printers from the paper were reportedly arrested for blocking military vehicles.

YANG Fang, an engineering student from Hefei in the mechanics department of Anhui Engineering Institute was arrested sometime in early July for "counter-revolutionary dissemination and incitement," according to a Hefei provincial radio broadcast (in *FBIS*, July 10, 1989). The radio report said he was chairman of the Student Autonomous Union of the Institute and a member of the provincical autonomous student federation in Hefei. He was allegedly responsible for organizing a boycott of classes at local universities, taking part in underground meetings and setting up road barricades to block traffic. According to a *UPI* report, the broadcast accused him of setting up a radio station called "Voice of the People" which, following the June 4 crackdown, broadcast Voice of America and various speeches that he personally recorded at Tiananmen Square, over speakers set up outside the city government building in Hefei. He was also accused of distributing pictures of the "alleged military crackdown." The Hefei Public Security Bureau has charged him with counter-revolutionary propagation and instigation.

LI Xiaohua and **ZHU Xiaotong,** both amateur writers, were arrested in mid-June, according to an Asia Watch source. Both were linked to the army. Li, about 35, was an editor of the People's Liberation Army Literature Publication House in Beijing and the winner of a national poetry award in 1988. He is believed to have been arrested in Guangzhou on June 12 after fleeing there from Beijing. Zhu was a young writer who used the pseudonym of Zhou Jiajun. He was a student at the University of Wuhan but was also affiliated with the 164th infantry battalion of the 55th army. He is believed to have been arrested in Wuhan.

WANG Zhengyun, one of the students on the government's "21 Most Wanted" list is reported by *Agence France Presse* to have been arrested sometime during the week of July 10. The arrest has not yet been confirmed by official sources. Wang, 21, is a native of Yunnan and a student at the Central Institute of Nationalities in Beijing. He is a member of an ethnic minority.

WANG Yan and **YANG Baikui,** associates of wanted political scientist Yan Jiaqi who has escaped from China through Hong Kong, were arrested probably around July 4 or 5.

LI Hui, a student leader, was arrested in June in Tianjin along with 45 others and accused of being a "counter-revolutionary rebel." According to a report in the *Tianjin Ribao* (June 17, 1989), Li was turned over on June 15 to the Beijing Municipal Public Security Bureau. The report termed Li the "general commander of the west line of Tiananmen Square under the Beijing Self-Governing Union of College Students" and said he had taken part in blocking military vehicles. It said he organized a propaganda team to go to Jinan and Wuhan to "stage counter-revolutionary instigation." On June 6, 1989, the report continued, Li and seven others arrived in Tianjin and began distributing leaflets

107

about "the true situation of the June 4 massacre."

According to a recent report in the *South China Morning Post* (October 25, 1989), **WANG Dan,** one of the top student leaders of the pro-democracy movement in Beijing, is still alive and reasonably well. A friend of Wang's has reportedly received a postcard from him, urging the friend to "keep up the effort." Wang was arrested on July 2 after meeting a Taiwanese journalist to ask for help in fleeing from China. Widespread fears were subsequently expressed that he had been badly beaten or even tortured to death in prison. Wang, 22, is a native of Jilin Province and a history student at Beijing University. A U.S. State Department spokesman reported in early February, 1990, that Wang had recently been visited in prison by his family.

Arrested with Wang was Peter T.P. HUANG, also known as **HUANG Teh-Pei,** a Taiwanese reporter for the *Independence Evening Post* in Taipei. Huang has since been released. He had reportedly just returned from a meeting with Wang, when he was picked up in front of his Beijing Hotel.

WANG Yang, Peter Huang's driver, was also arrested but has since been released.

LI Honglin, 63, a research fellow at the Fujian Academy of Social Sciences, was arrested at his home in Fuzhou, Fujian on July 6, 1989 according to the organization *Human Rights in China.* Ten armed police reportedly came to the house about 12 noon with both arrest and search warrants issued by the Public Security Bureau of Fujian Province. Officials at the Public Security Bureau refused to give the family information on where Li was being detained, saying they did not know. According to an Asia Watch source, Li has now been transferred to some form of "house arrest," though not at his home. Li had been an advocate of political and economic reforms and is the author of *The Storm of Theory*, summarizing the debate on socialism in China, and *Four Isms in China*. He had been head of the Research Institute of the History of the Chinese Communist Party at the Chinese History Museum and had been deputy director of the Bureau of Theory in the CCP's Propaganda Department. He was briefly president of the Fujian Academy of Social Sciences but resigned during the Anti Bourgeois Liberalization Campaign of 1986-87. He was one of 42 intellectuals who signed a letter to the Central Committee of the Communist Party on February 26, 1989 calling for the release of political prisoners.

ZHANG Cheng, a former student of Zhejiang Medical College, was arrested on June 15 by the Hangzhou City Public Security Bureau. According to a report on Hangzhou Radio (June 23, 1989; in *FBIS*, July 3, 1989) Zhang had been expelled from the college on theft charges but stayed on campus and became head of the autonomous student union there. According to the radio, he went to Beijing and returned with reactionary propaganda material, made speeeches and "orchestrated" attacks on railway stations and the blocking of trains. He is among 151 persons from 18 "illegal organizations" arrested thus far in Hangzhou, Ningbo, Wenzhou and Jinhua.

BAI Nansheng, Deputy Director of the Social Research Office of the Rural Development Research Institute, was reported arrested by *UPI* on July 10, 1989. His brother, BAI Nanfeng, an economist at the Research Institute for Reform of the Economic Structure, is also reported arrested. Individuals from both institutes had been implicated in a move to call an emergency session of the Standing Committee of the National People's Congress to abolish martial law.

SUN Changjiang, chief editor of *Beijing Keji Ribao*, was arrested on June 14, 1989 (*Zheng Ming*, October 1989).

WU Jiaxiang, a member of Anhui Province's central committee, was reportedly arrested on July 17, 1989; there has been no further word as to his whereabouts. Wu, formerly associated with ousted Party Secretary-General Zhao Ziyang and his close advisor, Bao Tong (now arrested, has been credited with applying Samuel Huntington's "new authoritarianism" to China. This theory would have provided a structure for centralizing power in the hands of one person.

The playwright WANG Peigong, 45, has been arrested in Guiyang (date not clear) according to the July 3 edition of *Wen Wei Po*. There has been no official confirmation of his arrest. Wang wrote a play called "WM" about the Cultural Revolution and had publicly renounced his membership in the Communist Party to show support for the democracy movement.

YUAN Chihe (who also apparently goes by the name Tasu), 23, the alleged chief director of the Beijing Autonomous Union of College Students of other Provinces, reportedly surrendered himself to the Baotou City Public Security Bureau on June 20. WANG Shufeng, 21, a student at Beijing University, and QIAN Shitun, described as core members of the same organization were also arrested on the same day. On June 21, Yuan and Wang were reportedly turned over to the Beijing Municipal Public Security Bureau for further investigation. Yuan, a student at the Baotou Teachers Training School, has been accused of having "incited, organized and directed students who came to Beijing from other provinces to engage in demonstrations, sit-ins and strikes." He was also reportedly interviewed by foreign reporters at Tiananmen Square, and after returning to Baotou, he allegedly "continued to spread rumors and to incite students to go on strike, engage in demonstrations and other illegal activities." WANG is accused of having once served as the chief director of a group of demonstrators from Beijing University, and was chief director of the hunger strike group of Tiananmen Square and chairman of the Tiananmen Square financial department. He was allegedly responsible for organizing and directing "illegal" student demonstrations, sit-in demonstrations, and hunger strikes. No biographical information or details about the charges against QIAN were reported. (Hohhot Inner Mongolia Regional Service, June 23, 1989; in *FBIS*, June 27, 1989.)

Forty-four people were reported arrested in Hebei province. **LIU Jian,** a Standing Committee member of the Autonomous Union of Beijing College Students, and **LIU Jianli,** "ruffian," were arrested on June 15 by the Xianghe County Public Security Department. **JI Funian,** a leader of the Autonomous Union of Beijing Citizens in charge of logistics; **WANG Zhigang,** a key member of the same organization; and three others (unnamed) were arrested on June 15 by the Xushui County Public Security Bureau. **ZHANG Jia,** head of the picket team of the Autonomous Union of the Beijing College Students was reported arrested on June 16 by the Shahe City Public Security Bureau.

YANG Yijun, 21, accused of setting ablaze 21 military vehicles during the "counter-revolutionary rebellion" in Beijing was arrested by the Qinhuangdao City Public Security Department on June 15. He was a student at a college associated with the Beijing Shoudu Iron and Steel Company and lived in Machangdian village, Niutouya township, Funing County. He had fled to Hebei Province after June 4 and was turned over to the Beijing Public Security Bureau after his arrest.

ZHONG Zhanguo, ZHANG Jianhua, and fourteen other staffers (unnamed) of the Harbin City Student Autonomous Federation of Higher Educational Institutions reportedly surrendered themselves to the Harbin City Public Security Bureau as of June 23. They reportedly handed over the stamps of their "unlawful" organizations and "presented the facts of unlawful activities committed since May 15 with regard to organizing students in higher educational institutions in Harbin City to strike and conduct street demonstrations, conduct petitions and set up road blocks in order to block workers from attending their production sites" (Harbin Heilongjiang Provincial Service, June 23, 1989; in *FBIS*, June 27, 1989).

ZHOU Guijin and ZHI Chengyi reportedly registered themselves with the Public Security Bureau of Shenyang City on June 22 and June 21, respectively. Zhou, 24, a student at the Shenyang Teachers Training School, is described as a member of the Shenyang City Autonomous Federation of College Students and general director of the "illegally-organized" Patriotic Society of Shenyang Teachers Training School. He reportedly directed a group of people to block traffic and roads on June 4, in order to prevent workers from getting to their jobs. On June 7, he also organized a group of people to go to the Shenyang airplane manufacturing company and the Shenyang instrument-making company to block the workers' route to work. Zhi is described as having been a liaison of the Shenyang City Autonomous Federation of College Students and vice chairman of an "illegal" organization of the China Medical College. He reportedly "accurately confessed to his illegal activities" (Shenyang Liaoning Provincial Service, June 23, 1989; in *FBIS*, June 27, 1989).

ZHAO Yiqiang, a teacher at Beijing Medical University, together with his wife and a graduate student at the university, were arrested in Zhangjiakou, 150 miles northwest of Beijing. They had reportedly assisted students involved in the hunger-strike (*Kyodo*, June 23, 1989; in *FBIS*, June 26, 1989).

SHI Jingang, a "major participant" in the pro-democracy movement, was arrested at a relative's home on June 10 by the Laoling City Public Security Bureau (Jinan Shandong Provincial Service, 22 June; in *FBIS*, June 23, 1989).

LIU Jianqiang, GUO Yonggang, and GONG Hui, natives of Beijing Municipality and "major participants" in the pro-democracy movement, were arrested on June 15 at the Dezhou railway station (Jinan Shandong Provincial Service, June 22, 1989; in *FBIS*, June 23, 1989).

YU Fangqiang, a student of the Beijing Science and Engineering University, and a "major participant" in the movement, was arrested in his native city of Xintai on June 17 (Jinan Shandong Provincial Service, June 22, 1989; in *FBIS*, June 23, 1989).

PAN Qiang, a leader in the Autonomous Union of Students of Colleges Outside Beijing, was arrested at Shandong University on the evening of June 20. PAN, a graduate of Shandong University's Foreign Literature Department, is reported to have led Shandong University's supporting group to Beijing on May 18. He is also reported to have served as a member of the liaison command

111

of the colleges of Shandong Province, and has been accused of participating in and plotting the "counter-revolutionary riot" (Jinan Shandong Provincial Service, June 22, 1989; in *FBIS*, June 23, 1989).

MA Shaohua, a native of Sichuan, was a student at the Chinese People's University, and a Standing Committee member of the Beijing College Students Autonomous Federation. He was arrested on June 16, in Zhigong Village of Baitian Township. He was reportedly in possession of "reactionary propaganda" at the time of his arrest (Changsha Hunan Provincial Service, June 19, 1989; in *FBIS*, June 20, 1989).

Two students of the Shanghai University of Science and Technology who were leaders of the Shanghai Autonomous Union of College Students, registered themselves with the Public Security Bureau in Jaiding County on June 14. WANG Hongming, 24, is in the University's Department of Precision Mechanical Engineering. SONG Mitu, 31, had graduated from the University in 1982 and is currently a graduate student in the Department of Radio (Shanghai City Service, June 16, 1989; in *FBIS*, June 20, 1989).

ZHOU Chifeng, liaison officer of the Sit-in Command at Tiananmen Square who had also been interviewed frequently by a *New York Times* reporter, was arrested by the Changchun City Public Security Bureau on June 12. He had been in hiding in Changchun, and was turned in to authorities by the Changchun Architecture College.

The same news dispatch reported that a student, unnamed, of the Jilin Industry University, who was head of the Organization Department of the Beijing Autonomous Union of College Students from Other Cities, recently turned himself in to public security organs and "confessed" to his activities in Beijing (Beijing Domestic Service, June 21, 1989; in *FBIS*, June 21, 1989).

As of June 15, 16 members of outlawed student and worker organizations in Nanjing were reported to have turned themselves in to the authorities. Those named were: HUANG Yongxiang, a Standing Committee member of the Autonomous Union of Nanjing Students and a post-graduate student of Nanjing University; and WU Jianlin, deputy commander-in-chief of the solidarity group in the north and a student of Provincial Institute of Business Management Cadres (Beijing Domestic Service, June 16, 1989; in *FBIS*; June 21, 1989).

According to the same dispatch, two others were arrested: WANG Yang*, Standing Committee member of the Autonomous Union of College Students and a student of the Nanjing Institute of Mechanical and Electrical Engineering, was arrested on June 14. **WANG Bin,** a member of the Autonomous Union of Beijing College Students was reportedly detained by the Public Security Bureau for interrogation, after he was discovered to be carrying "reactionary leaflets" and to have tried "to establish illicit ties in the Hehai University."

JING Wenqian (wrongly given as Jing Wenqing in AW Update, November 15), secretary of the Beijing Autonomous Students Federation and a graduate student of the Beijing Teachers Training University, has been tried and sentenced to between three and five years. According to an Asia Watch source, Jing, 26, arrested on June 15 for inciting people to intercept, burn and smash 31 military vehicles near the (Majia) Overpass in the Haidian Distiuct in Beijing, was originally held in Paoju Hutong Detention Center. **GUO Luxiang,** a student at the Department of Geology of the Beijing University, and **JIANG Xiaodong,** a student at the Beijing University of Science and Technology, arrested in Feicheng County on June 15 and escorted to Beijing on June 18, was accused in the same case. Jiang lived in the No. 7450 Plant in Feicheng and last year was admitted into Beijing University from the Feicheng No. 1 Middle School (Jinan Shandong Provincial Service, June 19, 1989; in *FBIS*, June 21, 1989).

On June 23, security officers arrested 17 students and teachers from several Beijing universities, including four from the Beijing Film Institute, ten from the Beijing Normal College of Physical Culture and one from the College of Politics and Law. There were reportedly warrants for 17 others. Their names have not yet been publicly announced.

LIU Xiaoqu, 27, and **LU Zhuru,** 29, two women accused of being involved in the democracy movement, were arrested at Beijing Airport sometime during the week of June 19 as they were preparing to board a plane for Paris. They were reportedly using passports that had been mailed to them from outside China, and a customs official spotted faked entry stamps (*South China Morning Post,* June 23, 1989).

WU Haizen, 34, a lecturer at the foreign language faculty of the Yunnan Education Institute, was arrested together with **YANG Hong** and **WANG Cun** on June 13 in Kunming, Yunnan for giving lectures "attacking party and government leaders" to students and workers. Wang Cun, 27, an accountant supervisor at the Kunming Jinglong Hotel, was accused of being head of propaganda for the Yunnan Students Federation. He "did a lot of evil through his contacts with Hong Kong and other regions," according to the radio. YANG Hong, 36, a reporter of a Kunming paper *Zhongguo Qingnian Bao,* was charged with

113

circulating "rumor-mongering leaflets" and protesting against corruption (Kunming Radio; in *FBIS*, June 16, 1989).

CHEN Yang, 22, a student at the Department of Law in the Politics and Law University in Beijing was arrested on June 15 in Shenyang, Liaoning Province. He was charged with being director of the Beijing Citizens' Autonomous Federation. A radio broadcast in Shenyang on June 17 said he had helped organize a "Dare-to-Die Corps," distributed "reactionary leaflets" and participated in "counter-revolutionary rebellion activities." He fled to Shenyang on June 9, and was arrested at his home by the Heping District Public Security Sub-bureau (*FBIS*, June 19, 1989).

ZHANG Weiping, 25, and CUI Jiancheng, 26, students of traditional Chinese painting at the Zhejiang Arts Faculty, were arrested on June 18 in Hangzhou. According to a Hangzhou radio report, Zhang was charged with incitement and counter-revolutionary propaganda for having telephoned Voice of America on June 6 to spread rumors that Hangzhou students were forcing the Zhejiang provincial government to lower its flag to half-mast in memory of the students killed in Beijing. The students apparently never succeeded in lowering the flag. In fact, they only succeeded in tearing it, according to the *New York Times* (June 21, 1989) which also suggested that Chinese security forces might have tapped the VOA line that Zhang called. Zhang was also accused of "wantonly uglifying" Chinese leaders by painting caricatures of them in late May, according to a *UPI* report. Zhang, reported to have "confessed" to all charges against him, was the first student known to have been tried since the crackdown began on June 4. He was sentenced on August 26, 1989 to nine years in prison by the Hangzhou Intermediate People's Court.

ZHANG Lin, director of the Autonomous Union of College Students in Bengbu City, was arrested there on June 8, according to a Hefei, Anhui radio broadcast (June 14, 1989). He had attended Qinghua University in 1985, according to the report, but was assigned the same year to work at the Bengbu Knitwear Mill. He had been unemployed since resigning from the mill at an unspecified date. The radio reported that he had established the Autonomous Union on May 19 at Bengbu Medical College and made an "extremely reactionary" speech on May 21. He also helped stage sit-ins and began a hunger strike on May 25, saying he wanted to turn Bengbu Medical College into a "center of democratic politics and to set up a human rights office at the college." He was said to have frequently traveled between Beijing and Bengbu beginning in

March 1989. In a letter he wrote which was apparently confiscated by authorities, he wrote of his intention to make contact with dissident astrophysicist, Fang Lizhi.

LIU Gang, 28, a physics graduate from Beijing University and one of the "21 Most Wanted" student leaders, was arrested in Baoding, south of Beijing on June 19, while trying to buy a railway ticket, according to a *UPI* report. Local residents turned him in after noticing that he did not have calloused hands as would have been expected from someone who wore the worker's clothing he did.

A London paper reported the arrest of the young student who stood in front of a tank column as millions watched on television. WANG Weilin, 19, the son of a factory worker was reported to have been arrested by secret police and charged with political hooliganism and "attempting to subvert members of the People's Liberation Army" (*London Express*, June 18, 1989). According to the newspaper account, friends of the young man recognized him after state television showed a line-up of detainees with their heads shaved.

Several arrests were reported following the June 13 broadcast on state television of "wanted posters" for 21 leaders of the student movement. MA Shaofang, 25, a student at the Beijing Film Academy and associate of student leader Wu'erkaixi, reportedy turned himself in on June 17 in Canton. YANG Tao, 19, a history student at Beijing University, who was also on the "most-wanted" list, was arrested in Lanzhou.

On June 18, state television announced the arrest of LI Xiuping, a young woman student leader, and YANG Zhiwei, both of whom were reported to have been detained in Baoding. Both had taken part in talks between the State Council and the independent student movement, according to the *Hong Kong Standard* (June 19, 1989).

A political science professor, WAN Xinjin, turned himself in in Shandong, apparently on June 18; he had been a leader of the Beijing Residents Autonomous Federation.

Four student leaders including CHEN Weitung and LIU Jiaming were arrested in Zhangjiakou over the weekend of June 17-18, and six students from the Autonomous Union of Beijing Universities and Colleges were arrested in Beijing.

On June 14, state television reported the arrest the day before of CHEN Xuedong, a student leader in Nanjing, who "organized several demonstrations, shouted reactionary slogans and wrote counter-revolutionary posters," according to the broadcast (*UPI*, June 15, 1989).

XIONG Wei, a student on the "21 Most Wanted" list reportedly turned himself in to the authorities on June 14 in the company of his mother. He had reportedly coordinated the medical teams helping those who staged the hunger strike in Tiananmen Square from May 13 until shortly before the crackdown.

Two other students on the "Most Wanted" list were arrested on June 13. ZHOU Fengsuo, 22, a physics major at Qinghua University was reportedly turned in by his elder sister and brother-in-law. He was arrested 90 minutes later by five policemen in Sanqiao, near Xi'an, and according to a *UPI* report, "confessed" that he was a member of the standing committee of the independent student union. Zhou had gone to Sanqiao from Beijing on June 7, according to one report (*South China Morning Post*, June 15, 1989).

XIONG Yan, 25, was a law student at Beijing University and was arrested on a train outside Datong, northeast of Beijing in Shanxi province. According to the *South China Morning Post* (June 15, 1989), he was one of a number of student leaders who had met with Premier Li Peng on May 18. At that meeting, he was quoted as saying, "We believe, no matter whether the government does or not, that history will recognize this movement as a patriotic and democratic movement...The people want to see whether the government is really a people's government or not." The arrests were announced by the government-controlled media.

On June 12, a student named FANG Ke, 33, turned himself in to the authorities in the city of Wuhan. He was a doctoral candidate in philosophy at Beijing People's University, and was said to be a member of the Standing Committee of the Autonomous Union of Beijing College Students, according to Beijing television (in *FBIS*, June 15, 1989).

The newspaper *Renmin Ribao* (June 13, 1989) reported the arrest in Xi'an of several student leaders. MA Hongliang, a leader of the Shaanxi Provincial College Students' Self-Government Federation and a student of the Xi'an Institute of Metallurgy, was arrested on June 7. A Xi'an radio broadcast on June 12 suggests that he was engaged only in peaceful protests: it said he had incited people against the provincial government, plotted to set up a radio station at Tiancheng Square in Xi'an to spread rumors and "poison people's minds" and instigated students and shopkeepers to strike. He had been active in Xi'an since mid-April.

Also mentioned by *Renmin Ribao* as having been arrested were **LIU Xiaolong, ZHU Lin, YU Yungang, LI Tao, PANG Xiaobin** and **WANG Jianjun,** members of a "Dare-to-Die" Contingent from Xi'an. The latter group were arrested at midnight on June 11 at a meeting in the Xingqinggong section of Xi'an City, according to the report. **WEI Yongbin,** another member, also was arrested (Amnesty International, June 16, 1989 release).

A liaison between students and workers named **ZHOU Shaowu** was arrested on June 10 in Shanghai, according to a June 14 broadcast of Beijing television. A former worker in the Ningguo County Ferro-Alloy Plant in Anhui, Zhou had been active in the Autonomous Union of Beijing College Students since May 18 when he had arrived in Beijing from Hefei. According to the broadcast, he had worked closely with another arrested student leader, Guo Haifeng (see index). He left Beijing on June 2 but did not arrive in Shanghai until June 6 where, according to the report, he made contact with counterpart organizations there. Among his possessions was a proposal to establish a "League of Democratic Parties" (in *FBIS*, June 15, 1989).

On June 10, Beijing Radio announced that **GUO Haifeng,** secretary-general of the United Association of Beijing Universities, had been arrested although the exact date of his arrest is not clear. The radio said he was captured "on the spot by the martial law enforcement troops while he and a gang of ruffians were trying to set fire to an Army unit's armoured vehicle." No other information about the circumstances of his arrest is available.

LIU Xiaobo, 34, is reported to have been arrested on Tuesday, June 6, when a man in plainclothes hustled him into a white car, according to eyewitness accounts. His arrest was only announced by the government on June 23. State radio, television and print media gave great prominence to the arrest and said Liu had close ties with Hu Ping, head of the U.S.-based organization Chinese Alliance for Democracy which publishes the journal *China Spring*. A native of Jilin province, Liu was a graduate of Jilin University and had just finished his doctoral dissertation at Beijing Normal University on the aesthetics of Chinese literature. Prior to his arrest he was on the faculty at Beijing Normal University. A well-known literary critic, Liu is the author of several books and articles, and once wrote for the *Shenzhen Youth Daily*. In April 1989, while visiting the United States, he published an article entitled "Contemporary Chinese Intellectuals and Politics" in which he strongly criticized some of the older Chinese intellectuals. He returned to China in late April to take part in the democracy movement. Following the declaration of martial law, he and three other activists began a hunger strike on June 2 at the base of the Monument of Revolutionary Heroes in Tiananmen Square. In a proclamation issued at the beginning of the strike, the four stated, "Through our hunger strike, we want also to tell the people that what the government media refers to as a small bunch of trouble makers is in fact the whole nation. We may not be students, but we are citizens whose sense of duty makes us support the democracy movement started by the college students...."

CHEN Mingyuan is believed to have been arrested June 10 or 11 although an arrest warrant for him was only issued ten days later. He is a professor at the Foreign Languages Institute in Beijing and taught Chinese to many foreigners resident there. He is also a mathemetician and a poet. He was taken to the hospital with high blood pressure and was reportedly arrested in the hospital. Chen was born in 1941 in Chongqing, Sichuan. He was imprisoned during the Cultural Revolution while working for the Chinese Academy of Sciences, after a book of poems billed as the "unpublished poetry of Chairman Mao" turned out to be his work. He is believed detained at the central office of the Public Security Bureau in Beijing.

REN Wanding is one of the few activists from the Democracy Wall movement period (1978-79) to have taken an active role in the 1989 demonstrations. The founder of the China Human Rights League, Ren was denounced together with Wei Jingsheng as a non-Marxist when the crackdown on the Democracy Wall movement came in 1979. He was arrested and spent four years in prison, his initial sentence having been extended when he refused to make an acceptable self-criticism. In 1988, he wrote an article for the *New York Times* on the tenth anniversary of Democracy Wall, calling on activist students to speak out for those in prison and on the business community to make any investment in China conditional on an end to suppression of dissidents. He is reported to have been arrested on June 9, about 8 p.m. His place of detention is not known.

WENG Zhengming, allegedly head of the China Youth Democracy Party (CYDP), was arrested on June 10. A self-employed tailor, according to Beijing Radio, he had established the party as early as 1986, arguing that an opposition party must emerge in China. After the student demonstrations began in April 1989, according to the radio, Weng went to several universities around Shanghai to recruit members for the CYDP. He had membership registration forms printed up together with a party platform. The party has been termed "counterrevolutionary" by the authorities.

LI Zhiguo was also arrested by the Shanghai Public Security Bureau around the same time, according to Beijing Radio (in *FBIS*, June 12, 1989). Beginning in March, according to the radio, he established the Freedom Society through which he advocated the founding of a "Kingdom of Greater Freedom." He "sent letters of comfort to troublemaking students in various localities and instigated them to fight the reactionary government to the end." According to the report, he also urged that a military camp be set up, and created a national flag, emblem, flower and currency for the new kingdom.

ZHU Wenli, 22, unemployed, was arrested in Shenyang, Liaoning on June 12, according to Liaoning Radio. He was captured by a staff member of the Heping Hotel in Shenyang after he tried to register at the hotel with a false identity card. The chief of the reception desk called security officials who found "materials for propagating counter-revolutionary rebellion" in his bag. According to the radio broadcast, he served as head of the social section of the Students Self-Governing Union of Beijing Colleges. He lived at the Tonghe Forest Farm in Weike Forest Bureau, Heilongjang Province.

YAO Yongzhan, 19, a student activist from Hong Kong, was arrested on June 11 at Shanghai Airport as he was getting ready to depart for Hong Kong on a Civil Aviation Administration of China (CAAC) flight. He was detained at the passport control section of the airport by about eight security officers, both uniformed and in plainclothes. British consular staff who accompanied him to the airport did not receive any response to their inquiries about his whereabouts or the charges against him. According to *Reuters*, Shanghai radio accused him of being the leader of the outlawed "Autonomous Union of Shanghai College Students" and said he was under investigation for violating local laws, including "carrying banned material." He was a first-year student in economics at Fudan University (*South China Morning Post*, June 13, 1989). His arrest was not officially acknowledged by Chinese authorities until July 28. He has been charged with "counter-revolutionary propaganda activities aimed at inciting the public" and will stand trial as a Chinese national.

Yao was born on February 16, 1970 in Shanghai. He finished elementary school in three years and began high school when he was twelve. In 1982 after mainlanders were allowed to settle in the British colony, he and his father moved to Hong Kong to live with Yao's mother. Yao was sent to private school, but after a year, he returned to Kongjiang High School in Shanghai, graduating in 1986.

Yao took the college entrance exams of China's seven specialized universities and was accepted at Fudan University's Management Science program when he was 16. He transferred to the economics program in 1988.

He should have returned to Hong Kong either in June or July 1989 to complete the formalities to qualify as a "Hong Kong belonger," a bonafide resident of the colony, but his arrest prevented him from doing so and he is being treated by Chinese authorities as a Chinese national.

The governments of Great Britain and Hong Kong have contacted Chinese authorities, urging Yao's immediate return to Hong Kong and warning against any maltreatment.

Neither Yao's father, Yao Wentian, a senior worker at a Tsuen Wan factory in Hong Kong, nor his mother have been allowed to see their son.

GUO Yanjun, a journalist working for the *Law Daily* (*Fazhi Ribao*) is reported to have been arrested in Beijing. The arrest has not been confirmed by Asia Watch.

A journalist, **GAO Yu,** vice-chief editor of *Economics Weekly,* is reported by reliable sources to have disappeared after June 4. She is thought to have been arrested by the authorities, rather than killed.

ZHANG Weiguo, a journalist for the *World Economic Herald* in Shanghai, was seized on June 20 and formally arrested September 20, 1989 on charges of counterrevolution. He is believed held incommunicado at No.1 Detention Center in Shanghai. Zhang reportedly undertook a one week hunger strike at a time he expected to be sentenced in secret without a trial. **XU Xiaowei,** also a *World Economic Herald* journalist, is believed held incommunicado at the same place. According to Hong Kong press sources, Xu was arrested in late June. Asia Watch has not been able to confirm his arrest, and there has not yet been official confirmation through the state media. The newspaper *Wen Wei Po* reported that Xu was accused of having worked with the Shanghai Autonomous Students Federation.

ZHANG Li, director of the publishing house of the Sichuan Provincial Academy of Social Sciences and **LI Jiawei,** editor of the publishing house, were expelled from the party for authorizing the publication of *The Complete Biography of Du Yuesheng.* (Du was a gangster in Shanghai in the 1930's who provided important support for Chiang Kai-shek.) The two men were accused of "seriously violating political discipline" and "departing from the orientation of socialist publication," according to a radio report in Chengdu, Sichuan broadcast on August 28. In addition to being expelled from the Communist Party, the men have probably also been arrested, as the radio report said they had violated provisions of the criminal code and that "the judicial organ is dealing with the matter according to law" (in *FBIS*, August 30, 1989).

CHEN Zhixiang, a teacher in Guangzhou, was sentenced to ten years' imprisonment for painting a "counterrevolutionary" slogan (US Department of State, *Country Reports on Human Rights Practices for 1989*, [Government Printing Office, February 1990], p. 807.)

5. ARRESTS OF CHINESE WORKERS AND PEASANTS

Asia Watch has learned that **HAN Dongfang,** 26, the leader of the Beijing Workers Autonomous Federation (BWAF), turned himself in to the authorities in Beijing in the latter part of June; he has been held incommunicado ever since. Han, before his arrest, was a railway worker in the Fengtai Locomotive Maintenance Section. He went into hiding on June 4, but was unable to remain underground for long. The BWAF was formed by a group of workers on May 19, the eve of the declaration of martial law; it was labeled as "counterrevolutionary" by the authorities on June 2, but was not formally declared to be illegal until June 8.

On June 14, the Chinese government issued a wanted notice for Han and two other leaders of the Federation, **HE Lili,** 26, formerly a lecturer at the Workers' University of the Beijing Bureau of Machinery Industry, and **LIU Qiang.** Liu, a worker at Factory No. 3209 in Beijing, was arrested later that day in Inner Mongolia; state television showed him being hauled off a train. He Lili's fate is not yet known.

Apart from a small, short-lived workers group which was set up in Taiyuan, Shanxi Province, in the winter of 1980, Han Dongfang's BWAF is thought to have been the first truly independent labor organization in China since the founding of the People's Republic. The BWAF's *Provisional Charter*, adopted in Tiananmen Square on 28 May 1989, made clear the organization's intention to operate openly and in full conformity with the laws and constitution of the PRC.

Until June 4, BWAF was based in two small tents, set up in the north-west corner of Tiananmen Square. Through a small broadcasting system there, they nightly transmitted items of news, commentary and political analysis which attracted audiences of several thousands, sometimes until dawn. Their tents were the first target of attack by the massive PLA force which arrived in the Square around 1:15 AM on June 4. Many of the BWAF's members and leaders, together with those of similar workers' organizations in other cities throughout China, have been rounded up and arrested in the subsequent crackdown, and the authorities appear to have reserved their harshest treatment for this category of detainees. Shortly before the crackdown, Han Dongfang said: "I'm not afraid. One can always find ways to survive. I just want us to be able to build an organization that can truly speak for the workers." For further details on Han, see chapter 3, above.

LI Hengjiang, 22, was arrested in Beijing in early January and charged with corruption, according to an Asia Watch source. Li worked in the Shangri-la Restaurant in Beijing and as a personnel assistant in a semi-private, semi-state company. On the authorization of the enterprise managers, but without the permission of the party, a contribution from company funds was made to the student movement, for which Li has been held responsible.

SHEN Yuehan, a member of the Beijing Workers Autonomous Federation and chairman of the official workers' union in the Bureau of Civil Engineering, has been arrested. Shen, approximately 30-years-old, is a resident of Beijing. The date and place of his arrest are uncertain.

WANG Guishen was arrested on December 4, 1989 in an eastern port city after being denounced by an informer. He is accused of "slandering" the Communist Party leadership and writing "counterrevolutionary" tracts which he posted throughout downtown Dalian. The official *Fazhi Ribao* of north-eastern Liaoning Province (January 6, 1990, in FBIS, January 16, 1990) said Wang, 38, harbored resentment against the party because, along with his father, he had been sent to the countryside during the Cultural Revolution (1966-76) for re-education among the masses.

WANG Langjie is awaiting trial as a "counterrevolutionary propagandist" according to the January 24 *Tibet Daily* (cited in *Reuters*, February 2, 1990). He is alleged to have wandered the environs of Beijing East Road, Lhasa, on January 5, yelling "Tibetan independence and other reactionary slogans." According to the press report, such behavior "is sufficient to constitute the crime of counterrevolutionary propagandist incitement."

PU Yong, 22, a medical worker and minor administrator in Nanjiang County, Sichuan Province, has been arrested in connection with "a major counter revolutionary propaganda and incitement case" (*Sichuan Ribao*; in *FBIS* November 1, 1989). Pu, who was elected as deputy director of Liangshui Township in May 1988 and was a worker at the Nanjiang County Hospital of Traditional Chinese Medicine, allegedly had "listened to the Voice of America, read reactionary publications and worshipped the capitalist social system prac-tised in Western countries." During the "counterrevolutionary rebellion," the high-school educated Pu had "posted big-character slogans in Nanjiang County and, on the night of October 29-30, he secretly wrote more than 400 counterrevolutionary leaflets which he distributed in 13 places in Nanjiang's downtown area, including bus stations, movie houses and the people's assembly hall." He also "took down and threw away the signboard of a government and party organ," and he "viciously attacked the Chinese Communist Party and China's socialist system and slandered its leaders."

ZHAO Shujian, 33, was arrested on November 7, 1989 for counter-revolutionary crimes allegedly committed on May 20 in Kaifeng in central Henan Province. According to *Henan Ribao* (December 3, 1989; in *FBIS*, December 15, 1989), Zhao, a cadre in the Kaifeng Housing Construction Company, painted more than 30 "reactionary" slogans on streets, schools and factories, organized illegal demonstrations, gave counterrevolutionary speeches at Henan University and spread the contents of Voice of America broadcasts at his own worksite during the height of the pro-democracy movement. He has been branded a "criminal" by the police, and accused of trying to "overthrow the Communist Party" and of having "viciously attacked and vilified state and party leaders." Zhao is alleged to have also written posters on earlier occasions, April 25, 1989 and January 18, 1987. He is said to have confessed to all his crimes.

FANG Xu, WANG Chunfu, both workers, and CHEN Minchun, unemployed, were convicted for crimes allegedly committed during the pro-democracy demonstrations in Nanjing (*Jiangsu Fazhi Bao*; in *FBIS*, November 20, 1989). Fang and Wang, who allegedly had previous records for theft, were sentenced to seven years each by a Nanjing court for forcing two drivers from their vehicles on May 18 in Nanjing and for wounding passersby who tried to stop them. Fang was also convicted of attacking a vendor with a knife the following day. Chen, was sentenced to five years for provoking fights during May and June, resulting in injury to six people at a town market. He too is alleged to have a criminal record.

WANG Jiaxiang and WANG Zhaoming were sentenced by a Beijing court on December 7, 1989 for spreading "counterrevolutionary propaganda" and "inciting" rebellion. Neither the dates of their arrests nor the terms of their sentencing have been reported (*South China Morning Post*, December 15, 1989).

ZHANG Jingsheng and Wang Changhuai, alleged "counterrevolutionary criminals" were sentenced on December 7, 1989 by the Changsha Intermediate People's Court in a special urban meeting (in *FBIS*, December 14, 1989). According to the official *Hunan Ribao* dated December 9, Zhang, 35, a former Democracy Wall activist, received a thirteen year sentence and was deprived of his political rights for three years. He had previously served four years for spreading "counterrevolutionary propaganda." Wang, 25, was given a three year sentence for turning himself in on June 15 and was deprived of his rights for one year. Wang, formerly a worker at the Changsha Automobile Engine Factory, had been head of Changsha's Workers Autonomous Federation and its propaganda section chief. Zhang, a casual laborer in a factory in Shaoguan, Hunan province, is said to have made speeches on May 4, 1989 at Hunan University and at the Changsha Martyrs' Mausoleum calling for the release of Wei Jinsheng, the Democracy Wall activist. On May 21, Zhang joined the Workers Autonomous Federation. He allegedly incited workers to go on strike and students to boycott classes. After the crackdown in Beijing, he wrote a letter of appeal, distributed by the Workers Federation, urging that fighting against the government continue. This is Zhang's second had served a four year prison term for spreading "counterrevolutionary propaganda."

Two Shanghai workers, **JIANG Xidi** and **ZHANG Jinfa,** accused of joining the counter-revolutionary riot in June in Shanghai, were reportedly sentenced to 12 and 11 years respectively. Neither the dates of arrest nor of sentencing are known.

LIU Chengwu, a Shenyang resident, was arrested on October 30 for "openly propagating reactionary words and disrupting public order." According to the report in *Liaoning Fazhi Bao* (November 7, 1989), the 25-year-old unemployed Liu, who served a prison sentence for theft in 1983-85, set up a radio outside his mother's restaurant on June 7 to transmit Voice of America news about the Beijing massacre. "Many people stopped to listen to the radio. As a result traffic was seriously disrupted."

GAO Hao and **WANG Baikun** were arrested in Shanghai in November for their role in the June demonstrations (*Washington Post*, December 3, 1989). Gao was seized at the Shanghai railroad station on November 7 for burning military vehicles during "the counterrevolutionary rebellion" in Beijing. Wang, identified as a leader of a Dare-to-Die brigade that provided security for students during the "period of turmoil," was captured on November 16.

Reuters reported on October 11 that a peasant had been jailed in Canton for blocking traffic and demonstrating in early June under a banner that read "Workers of Canton." He was sentenced to five years, but his name was not mentioned.

Five people were sentenced to imprisonment by the Xi'an People's Court

126

on September 23-24, according to reports in the Hong Kong newspaper, *Ming Bao* (September 26). According to the *Xi'an Evening News* (*Xi'an Wanbao*, September 22, 1989), those convicted were **FENG Shuangqing**, a worker at a pharmaceutical plant in Xi'an; **YU Yong**, a worker; **LIU Gang***, identified as an unemployed worker; and **ZHAO Ping**, a peasant. The name of the fith is not known. Liu Gang, not to be confused with a student leader of that name who is also under arrest, was sentenced to life imprisonment, according to the paper.

MENG Jinquan, 22, accused of burning seven military vehicles and raping a woman during the "counter-revolutionary rebellion" in Beijing, was arrested by the Wanzhuang Security Inspection Station of the Langfang City Public Security Bureau on June 15 (Beijing Domestic Service, June 20, 1989; in *FBIS*, June 27, 1989.)

DONG Shengkun, MIAO Deshun, WANG Guoqiang, SHI Guoquan and **ZHAI Yicun** were arrested on charges of engaging in violent acts and instigating "counterrevolutionary protests" in Beijing following the June 4 crackdown, according to *Beijing Ribao* (June 27, 1989). Dong, Miao, and Wang were accused of setting a fire; Shi and Zhai were accused of looting. **ZHANG Jianzhong**, 26, allegedly a member of the "Dare-to-Die Corps," and **BAI Xinyu**, 60, allegedly a Taiwan soldier and KMT agent, were also reported arrested in connection with the same case. Zhang, a former Beijing worker and allegedly a bodyguard for leaders of the Beijing Students Autonomous Federation and for the broadcast station "Voice of the Student Movement," was charged with mutilating the body of **LIU Guogeng**, a soldier killed in the army's June 5 assault on the student demonstrators; Bai, who had previously served a 15 year sentence for murder, was said to have burned a military vehicle. Two others arrested at the same time, Li Wenbao and Liang Hongchen (see Executions) were sentenced to death and are believed to have been executed (*UPI*, June 27, 1989).

LIN Qiang and **WANG Liqiang** have been tried by a Beijing District Court for attempts to incite workers at the Capital Iron and Steel Company to join the democracy protests on May 20, according to *Beijing Wanbao* (Beijing Evening News, July 6, 1989). Two drivers from Beijing arrested in the same case, **YI Jinyao**, 20, who was assigned to a Beijing City government office, and **TAN Minglu**, received sentences of four years and three-and-a-half years respectively. The report said both tried to persuade steel workers to help set up blockades to prevent troops from moving into the city on the day martial law was declared. Yi, a driver with a Beijing city government office, was sentenced to 4 years in prison, and TAN was sentenced to three-and-a-half years by a Beijing District Court.

BAI Wenbo was arrested on June 11, according to *Beijing Ribao* (June 13, 1989) for allegedly burning a military vehicle and giving a "counter-revolutionary" speech. No further details are available.

On the same day *Beijing Ribao* reported two additional arrests: YU Peiming, 59, a Beijing steel worker, who gave a speech in the Liuliqiao area allegedly criticizing Party leaders and inciting people to overthrow the government; and YU Tieliang, unemployed, said to have attacked soldiers and burned vehicles on June 3. Both were arrested on June 11.

CHEN Qisheng and HE Wensheng were also reported to have been arrested sometime after June 11 for hiding a submachine gun on June 6 (*Beijing Ribao*, July 4, 1989). Both men were members of the Black Panther Shock Brigade of the Beijing Citizens Autonomous Federation.

Twelve people arrested on June 12 in Daxing County near Beijing include SUN Yanru (possibly a woman); ZHANG Guojun; LI Huanxin, a worker at Zhongmei Model Flour Factory; XIE Nanfang, a driver at the Capital Bus Company; HE Yongpei, a worker at the Wangfujing Art Store; GAO Hong, a service worker at the Yongdingmeng Motel; and CHEN Yonggang, an operator at the Dongdan Telephone Bureau. They were accused of destroying military vehicles, attacking the police and spreading rumors (*Beijing Ribao*, June 14, 1989).

SONG Zhengsheng and GAO Liuyou were tried in Beijing Intermediate Court for burning military vehicles. There are no further details available (*Beijing Ribao*, July 1, 1989).

Shanghai resident GENG Xiuchong, 30, was accused on June 5 of "faking a bloody cloth as evidence of the Beijing massacre," according to *Beijing Ribao* (June 29, 1989).

LI Mou, an employee of the Merchant and Industry Station at Huilongguan, Changping County and a Beijing Workers "Dare-to-Die" Corps member, was arrested on June 13, 1989 in Huoying, Changping County near Beijing for joining the June 3-4 riots (*Beijing Ribao*, June 15, 1989). PANG Fuzhong, a peasant from Shanxi Province, was arrested a day later in Beijing for burning military vehicles on June 4.

SUN Hong, 18, a worker at a fluorescent light factory in Beijing, was turned in to the authorities by an informer (date unknown). He is said to have burned military vehicles and stolen a gun on June 4-5 (*Beijing Ribao*, June 15, 1989).

SUN Baochen, BAI Zenglu, and MA Jianxin, all from Dingxian County, Hebei Province, were arrested on June 6 in Zhuozhou City (*Zhongguo Qingnian Ribao* [China Youth Daily] June 14, 1989) for allegedly joining the "counter-revolutionary" protest in Beijing.

GAO Feng, who is alleged to have gone from Beijing to Xi'an on May 19 to stir up people and urge them to initiate a hunger strike in Xingcheng Square, has been arrested (date unknown). According to a report in *Zhongguo Qingnian Ribao* on July 1, 1989, Gao, who is unemployed, spread rumors on May 20 and 22 at Northwestern Industry University and pretended to be a *Zhongguo Qingnian Ribao* reporter.

Two brothers, CHENG Honglin, a Beijing worker, and CHENG Hongli are reported to have been arrested for a June 3 attack on the police *(Beijing Wanbao*, June 21, 1989). The dates of their arrests are unknown.

HUO Liansheng, 22, a peasant from Miyun County east of Beijing, was arrested on June 4 and accused of stealing a gun (*Beijing Wanbao*, June 10, 1989).

LI Zixin, a 20-year-old peasant from Dongzhao Village, Fashang Brigade, Daxin County near Beijing, was arrested for having joined a group attempting to stop military vehicles on May 22, according to *Beijing Wanbao* (June 3, 1989).

SONG Kai, a 34-year-old service worker at Yanjing Drugstore in the West District of Beijing, turned himself in to the police, admitting only to minor misconduct. He was formally arrested on June 17, on charges of stopping and attacking soldiers on June 4 (*Beijing Wanbao*, July 6, 1989).

CAO Qihui, a Beijing worker and a member of the motorcycle team which supported students during pro-democracy activities, is reported by *Tuanjie Bao* (September 5, 1989) to have been arrested on July 8.

CAO Yingyun, 36, a worker at the Second Machine Tool Factory in Beijing, is reported to have been arrested in the Fengtai district on May 24, 1989 as he destroyed slogans that supported Li Peng and spread material that "attacked the leader of the Party and the government" (*Beijing Wanbao*, June 3, 1989).

SUN Feng, a worker who joined the student demonstrations on May 14 and was in charge of the Beijing Students Autonomous Federation's broadcasting station, was arrested on June 2 along with WANG Wei. Sun is charged with spreading rumors, blocking traffic and disturbing the social order (*Beijing Ribao*, June 4, 1989).

WANG Gang, 27, manager of the Jinlong Hotel in Kunming was arrested and charged with "counterrevolutionary propaganda" and contacting people from Hong Kong. (See WU Haizen.) The date of his arrest is uncertain; Wu, however, was arrested on June 13, 1989.

ZHENG Jinli, unemployed, is reported to have been arrested in Dalian on June 13 along with JIAO Zhixin and SONG Tianli. Zheng was allegedly a leader of a "counterrevolutionary organization" (*Zhongguo Qingnian Ribao*, June 14, 1989; Amnesty International Urgent Action: 202), as were Song, unemployed, and Jiao, a salesman. The three allegedly formed the China Democratic Political Party during the student demonstrations and advocated the overthrow of the Chinese Communist Party and the socialist system (AI Urgent Action 202/89, June 22, 1989).

ZHU Lianyi, a worker of the Third Urban Construction Company in Beijing, was arrested on June 8 after being turned in by informers. Four others including GUO Yaxiong, a member of the Self-governing Union of Workers of Beijing Municipality, were arrested at the same time according to a Beijing television broadcast of June 14. Zhu reportedly joined the Beijing Workers Autonomous Federation on May 18 and was in charge of setting up its printing workshop (*Beijing Wanbao*, June 22, 1989). Guo, a native of Hunan, drafted a "Declaration of the Dragon" and "distributed it here and there in an effort to egg on people to make trouble."

ZHANG Jie, 22, an unemployed worker from Jinan, Shandong Province, was recently sentenced to 18 years' imprisonment for making counterrevolutionary speeches, according to a report in the *Jinan Masses Daily* on October 15. Zhang's crime was that he had stood outside the municipal government offices in Qingdao on June 5 and called upon a crowd of several thousand people to hold mourning activities for the dead in Beijing.

SUN Xiongying, 24, was sentenced to 18 years in prison by the Intermediate People's Court of Fuzhou City, Fujian province for "counterrevolutionary sabotage and demagoguery" (Fuzhou Fujian Provincial Service, December 21, 1989, in FBIS, January 12, 1990). The charges were said to carry sentences of 12 and seven years, but the court required he serve a total of "only" 18 years; he was deprived of his political rights for five years. Sun, formerly a cadre at the training office of the Fuzhou City Sparetime University, allegedly "engaged in the counterrevolutionary activities of writing reactionary slogans and defacing and damaging the statues of leaders." He reportedly smeared black paint on a statue of Mao in front of the Workers' Cultural Palace in Fuzhou and on the name plate of the Fuzhou City People's Government. He also scribbled reactionary slogans at Wuyi Square Park and Xiamen University. (In July, three men accused of throwing ink and paint-filled eggshells at Mao's portrait in Tiananmen Square in May were sentenced to prison terms ranging from 16 years to life. See index: **LU Decheng, YU Dongyue** and **YU Zhijian.**)

Two unemployed men, **LI Jueming** and **LI Jinhua**, and a peasant named **ZENG Weidong**, were sentenced on October 9 by the Guangzhou Intermediate Court to prison terms of 18, 13 and 5 years for acts allegedly committed by them after June 4. According to a report issued by the *China News Agency* (October 9, 1989), the two Li's "took advantage" of the student demonstrations in Guangzhou's Haizhu Square to intercept and damage a total of 15 vehicles, and to "openly insult" two young women who were passing through Haizhu Square. Zeng Weidong was sentenced for having gone to Haizhu Square on the night of June 6 and "joining a group of people who were waving the banner of "Guangzhou Workers." It is also alleged that while there, he took part in acts of "beating, smashing and looting."

LI Xinfu (Xingfu) and **CHEN Jiahu**, both seized in late August along with "counterrevolutionary" programs, letters and members' registration forms, have been sentenced to long prison terms "for organizing a counterrevolutionary party," China's Savior Party, in 1988 in the Wuchuan Gelao-Miao Autonomous County in Guizhou Province (*Renmin Gongan Bao*; in *FBIS* November 3, 1989; *Fazhi Ribao* in *FBIS* November 7, 1989). Ten other leaders and core activists have also been arrested and put on trial according to the *People's Public Security News* (*FBIS*, November 3, 1989). The twelve were described as being "mainly counterrevolutionaries and criminal offenders who continued to oppose the people after being discharged from prison." Li and Chen had served previous prison sentences for organizing a "counterrevolutionary party." The China Savior Party reportedly involved a total of 118 people from four counties and 28 towns, and the accused were charged with having "forged central documents and cheated people out of more than 7,000 yuan in cash by means of purchasing counterrevolutionary money and shares." However, the main charges were apparently related to the pro-democracy movement: "In May of this year, while turmoil occurred in the whole nation, Li Xinfu went to Chongqing to watch the situation and to collect and copy leaflets, and he encouraged core members to 'put objectives and aspirations into practice'."

The Public Security Bureau of Wuchuan Gelao-Miao Autonomous County in Guizhou is credited with having cracked the case under the leadership of higher public security organizations, and with the cooperation of police bureaus from Meiyun, Zhengan and Fenggang counties.

In another such case in Guizhou Province, an unspecified number of local farmers were arrested recently after allegedly forming a "dissident party" aimed at toppling the Communist Party. According to a report in the *People's Public Security News*, the dissident party had plotted to attack public security organizations' arsenals, blow up bridges and cut telephone lines on August 20, but the plot was detected and the party's leaders arrested on October 10 (in *FBIS*, October 30, 1989).

On October 29, the China News Service reported that **DAI Weiping** and three other men (unnamed) had been arrested in Chongqing, Sichuan Province, for allegedly belonging to a dissident ring, the "Chongqing Patriotic and Democratic Alliance." The organization had allegedly been formed on May 21 and had continued its activities even after the government's military supression of the pro-democracy movement in Beijing. After June 4, Dai Weiping and his followers "held secret meetings, planned the formation of 'underground armed forces, attempted to seize and steal firearms and ammunition and even tried to seek support from overseas forces." No other details about the men were given, but the Hong Kong press has quoted provincial sources as saying that the "Chongqing Patriotic Democratic Association" was a workers' organization with some support from the unemployed.

The *Legal Daily* reported recently that an unidentified peasant from Tianzhen had been sentenced to 10 years for engaging in "counterrevolutionary provocation." He had reportedly travelled to Beijing with a group of students to participate in pro-democracy demonstrations in May, and upon his return had demonstrated with students in Jinan and given "reactionary" lectures in his home village (in *FBIS*, November 3, 1989).

SUN Jizhong, a brick factory worker, was arrested in Beijing on September 28, 1989 after returning from North Korea. After taking part in a "Dare to Die" brigade in Beijing on May 31 which tried to block military trucks from entering the city after martial law was declared, Sun fled to Tumen in Jilin Province and then crossed illegally into North Korea, according to a report in the Beijing Evening News (*Reuters*, October 12, 1989).

The trial of 14 "counter-revolutionaries," all accused of having stolen guns from troops during the government crackdown against the pro-democracy movement on June 4, was broadcast on Chinese television on September 8, according to *Reuters*. Seven men, their heads shaven, received sentences ranging from two to thirteen years imprisonment. Among these, **MENG Fangjun** was jailed for 13 years for stealing a machine gun from a burned out tank and then hiding it at home; two brothers who helped him were each jailed for 10 years. The other seven accused were told they would be released as they had surrended to the police.

TIAN Bomin, 24, a member of the Beijing Workers Autonomous Federation, was arrested in Yunnan together with 36 others who had fled Beijing, according to Agence France Presse in an August 4, 1989 dispatch. He is believed to have been arrested between June 4 and July 8. Some of those arrested were reportedly trying to flee China.

XIAO Shifu, LI Lixin and **LIN Weiming** were arrested on July 15 in Guangzhou. Xiao and Li are accused of trying to use fake Singaporean passports to flee the country; Lin, a Hong Kong resident, is accused of providing the passports for HK$300,000.

In its August 17 update, Asia Watch reported the sentencing of **RUI Chaoyang** and **ZHANG Bingbing** for their part in a riot that broke out in Xi'an following a memorial service for deposed Communist Party Secretary Hu Yaobang. Rui Chaoyang was sentenced to life imprisonment for "hooliganism." He was found guilty of breaking into a government compound, throwing stones at police and smashing windows of a tourist bus, according to a Reuter release of August 17. Zhang Bingbing was sentenced to 16 years. An account of their arrest and trial was reported over Beijing radio on August 16. According to that report, Rui Chaoyang was a temporary worker of the Xi'an (Huanbao) Boiler Company. Zhang Bingbing was a contract worker of the installation team of the Shaanxi Provincial No.3 Construction Company.

Five others were also tried and sentenced by the Xi'an Intermediate People's Court for their involvement in the April 22 riot. **FAN Changjiang**, unemployed, was sentenced to 12 years for stealing audio tapes and looting a clothing store. The other four, **WANG Zunning** and **XIAO Sanfeng,** both peasants from Lantian County; **ZHAO Jian**, a temporary worker of the Xi'an Institute of Metallurgical and Architectural Engineering; and **SUN Chaohui**, a temporary worker in the Chengzhong office of the Employment Service Company of the Xi'an Survey and Drawing School were sentenced to three to four years in prison for "disrupting social order."

CHEN Ting and **LIANG Jianshe,** deputy heads of the Workers Volunteer Brigade in Hefei, Anhui, were arrested in Wenzhou, Zhejiang Province. The date of arrest is not clear. Both had apparently been active in demonstrations that rocked Hefei between June 4 and June 9, 1989.

YANG Jianhua was arrested by authorities in Dachang Hui Nationality Autonomous County for burning 30 military vehicles during the "counter-revolutionary rebellion," according to *Hebei Ribao.*

DING Peilin and **DING Jie,** father and son, were arrested for allegedly beating martial law enforcement troops during the crackdown in Beijing. Both were arrested in Xingtai City, Hebei, according to *Hebei Ribao* (July 12, 1989).

ZHAO Yude, described in the same report only as a "ruffian," was accused of attacking public security cadres. He was arrested by the Jixian County Public Security Bureau in Hebei.

QI Minglian, a worker, was arrested in Jiangsu Province after returning home from Beijing where he had reportedly stolen military property during the crackdown on unrest in the capital on June 3-4. He was among the 3,782 arrested in that province.

LI Nianbing, YU Chunsheng, WAN Yong, WAN Guoping and **WANG Zhongshou** were jailed in southern Jiangxi province for "serious" public order offenses committed in the square of the provincial capital Nanchang during a demonstration there on May 4. According to the July 20 *Jiangxi Daily*, the five blocked traffic, smashed and overturned vehicles, set fire to property and attacked people. Li Nianbing, a worker, was jailed for four years. Yu Chunsheng, identified only as a company employee, Wan Yong, jobless, and Wan Guoping, a worker, were jailed for three years. Wang Zhongshou, self-employed, received a two year sentence.

LI Shiqian, a worker at a Beijiao farm near Beijing, was shown on state television June 22 with a pistol his son allegedly had taken from a soldier and used during the student demonstrations in Tiananmen Square, where he was deputy leader of a "Dare-to-Die" team. Li Shiqian was arrested on June 20 for having hid the pistol, money, and walkie-talkies. His son, also named LI, fled Tiananmen Square on June 4 and buried the articles on the grounds of the farm, according to a report in *Beijing Ribao* (June 23, 1989). The son was arrested on June 13. Public security officials attempted many times to "persuade" Li Shiqian to turn over the articles. Instead he reburied them in another place where they were found and confiscated by the authorities.

WU Qiang, a 22-year-old worker, was arrested in Beijing on July 2, 1989 and convicted of stealing firearms. On June 6, the Beijing Municipal People's Procuratorate claimed, Wu threw bricks and soft drink bottles at three military vehicles. On the following day, according to the court, he looted firearms from a burned tank. Because Wu had refused to surrender, according to a report on Beijing radio, he will be strictly punished.

LIU Yihai, a worker of Trucking Unit #5 of the Harbin City Bus Transport Company, was among 33 people arrested on June 6 by the Harbin City Public Security Bureau according to a Jinhua radio broadcast. He was accused of having been part of a group of 38 "unlawful elements" who shouted at students, threw sand and rocks at trucks and tried to protest in front of the Public Security Bureau itself. A report in *Heilongjiang Ribao* (June 9, 1989) said the group appeared at Harbin Civil Engineering College, Harbin Shipbuilding College and Harbin Engineering College at 11 p.m., seriously disturbing students' sleep. Liu Yihai had a criminal record for pick-pocketing, according to the report. It said he confessed to joining in the incident to "vent his spite upon the government." He is also accused of robbing trucks in the Nangang District of Harbin City. He said he did so "because he hated the government," according to the radio report.

FENG Guowei and **YE Fuzhan** were arrested in Tianjin sometime in mid-June, according to a report in *Tianjin Ribao* (June 12, 1989). Both had recently been released from labor camps. They were accused of taking part in a "Residents Support Group" for the student demonstrators and gathering in front of colleges and universities to shout "reactionary slogans." Feng and Ye do not appear to have been themselves charged with violent acts. A third person arrested at the same time, **JIA Changling** from Siping City, was reported to have "openly incited some people to storm department stores, smashing glass and narrowly avoiding major incidents."

XU Guocai, a peasant from Songjiaguo village, Huanhe township, Tieling County, Shenyang was arrested for sending 13 counter-revolutionary letters between April 20 and May 26. Signed in the name of the "special administrative team of the Northeast China Joint Forces for Saving the Country," they called on military districts in the region to overthrow the government, stage mutinies and support student unrest, according to a provincial radio broadcast.

TANG Yuanjun was arrested in Changchun, Jilin Province on June 10, together with five other workers in the engine branch plant of the Changchun No.1 motor vehicle plant, an automobile factory. **LI Wei and LENG Wanbao,** are two of those arrested. Over the past two years, according to a Jilin provincial radio broadcast (in *FBIS*, July 10, 1989) they recruited 11 other workers and "instigated workers to go on strike and organized illegal demonstrations." According to a July 19th *UPI* report, a local radio broadcast said all six had been part of a "counter-revolutionary clique" which was planning a city-wide strike designed to "topple the socialist system."

CAO Zihui, a worker at the Beijing Motor Vehicle and Motorcycle Plant, was arrested with Li Hui (see index) in Tianjin on June 7. The report in *Tianjin Ribao* also said he was a member of the "Northeast Tiger Dare-to-Die Team" and someone who had seized two soldiers from the People's Liberation Army and brought them to Tiananmen Square "for publicity."

LUAN Zhetang was arrested at Tianjin Station about the same time as Li Hui and Cao Zihui. A worker at the Jining Textile Machinery Plant in Shandong, he was accused of smashing military vehicles and beating the corpses of dead soldiers in Beijing on June 4.

ZHOU Liwei, unemployed, was also arrested in Tianjin; he was said to be a bodyguard for the autonomous student federation in Beijing. The reference to him in *Tianjin Ribao* (June 13, 1989) did not suggest he had been involved in violence.

LI Yongsheng, arrested in Tianjin on or around June 11, was said to have organized the "Tianjin residents' petitioning team" and to have engaged in "rumor-mongering" at Nanyuan Airport, according to the *Tianjin Ribao* report. He was unemployed.

WANG Jinji, occupation unknown, was also arrested in Tianjin on June 10 and accused of collecting funds for the students, according to Amnesty International.

In Chengdu, Sichuan, **CHENG Yong, NI Erfu** and **ZHANG You** were sentenced to life imprisonment on July 8, 1989, according to *Agence France Presse*. At their trial, on charges of taking part in the riots which swept Chengdu after the Beijing massacre, the death sentences of Wang Guiyang and Zhou Xiangcheng (see index) were upheld.

ZHAO Yasui, 28, was arrested in Beijing for beating soldiers and stealing a rifle, according to the Beijing Evening News. The arrest was reported in a *UPI* release (July 8, 1989), but the date of Zhao's arrest is not clear. It apparently took place in connection with the recent protests.

LIANG Zhenyun, a self-employed auto mechanic, was reported by the Beijing Evening News to have been arrested for taking a machine gun and a pistol from a soldier on June 4, according to a *UPI* report (July 14, 1989).

GUO Guihong, 26, and **WANG Xia** were sentenced on June 29 by the Shanghai Railway Transportation Court to five and four years respectively for disrupting traffic during demonstrations in Shanghai on June 5 and 6. The sentences were announced by Shanghai Radio as reported by *FBIS* (July 7, 1989). Gao Guihong, self-employed, had previously been detained for "scuffling," according to the broadcast. He was charged with gathering crowds to stop three passenger trains at a railway crossing near Guangxin Road and with stopping the vehicles near the same spot. Wang Xia worked at the Shanghai No. 7 Weaving Mill. She was accused of inciting people to sit on railway tracks during a demonstration in Shanghai on June 6. The broadcast said she had previously served time in re-education for "hooliganism."

Three men accused of smearing the giant portrait of Chairman Mao in Tiananmen Square on May 23, 1989 by flinging ink and paint-filled eggshells (*South China Morning Post* , July 2, 1989) have been tried and sentenced by the Intermediate Court in Beijing. **YU Zhijian,** aged 25, was sentenced to life imprisonment, **YU Dongyue** to 20 years and **LU Decheng,** aged 26, to 16 years for "counter-revolutionary destruction and counter-revolutionary incitement." They had been charged with "counter-revolutionary" incitement and sabotage. The charges were filed on June 30 at the Beijing Municipal Intermediate People's Court. Yu Zhijian was a teacher at the Tantou Primary School in Dahu Township, Liuyang country, Hunan; Yu Dongyue was an art editor for a newspaper organization called *Liuyang Bao*; and Lu Decheng worked for the Liuyang Branch of the Hunan Provincial Bus Company, according to a Xinhua News Agency Report on June 30. The three had come to Beijing on May 19 from Changsha where they had made anti-government banners and had given "counter-revolutionary" speeches, according to the report.

On June 23, the Huangpu District People's Court sentenced 14 members of a Shanghai "Dare-to-Die Corps" to prison terms for allegedly obstructing traffic, deflating tires and beating drivers during demonstrations in Shanghai. **DAI Zhong,** was sentenced to a term of 3 to 7 years. **ZHAN Xinhuo** (ZHAN Xinguo) and **YUAN Zhiqiang** (YAN Zhiqiang) were sentenced to 8 years imprisonment, and deprived of their political rights for one year. **TANG**

Jianzhang was sentenced to 13 years and deprived of his political rights for 3 years; **CHEN Honggen** was sentenced to 11 years and deprived of his political rights for 2 years (Shanghai City Service, June 24, 1989; in *FBIS*, June 27, 1989).

A peasant named **REN Yingjun** was reportedly arrested sometime in June for throwing rocks at the headquarters of the Ministry of Radio, Television and Film in Beijing on June 4, according to the *Beijing Daily*.

According to the June 29 issue of *The Legal News*, **ZHANG Chunhui**, 24, was arrested in Beijing. He was accused of helping to kill a soldier during the unrest (*Reuters*, June 30, 1989).

Six "principal" members of the "Xi'an Workers Picket Corps" were arrested (date not given) and "brought to justice." **AN Baojing** and **ZHAO Demin** had been accused of setting up the organization and of having "instigated" a group of people to stage demonstrations in Xi'an City, by "yelling reactionary slogans and spreading reactionary leaflets." They were also accused of blocking traffic on June 4, 5, and 6. Charges against **REN Xiying, XU Ying, BAO Hongjian, CHANG Ximing** were not described in the report, although it stated that "the six criminals have candidly confessed their illegal acts committed since the second half of May" (Xi'an Shaanxi Provincial Service, June 25, 1989; in *FBIS*, June 27, 1989).

WANG Changan, 21, a worker, was arrested after turning himself in to local authorities. He has been accused of setting up barricades on roads and railway tracks (*Agence France Presse*, June 24, 1989; in *FBIS*, June 26, 1989).

The *Beijing Daily* reported that **LI Bing**, a leader of a Beijing worker's independent organization, was arrested in Beijing on June 21 for allegedly killing a soldier, and for trying to block military vehicles from entering Tiananmen Square (*Kyodo*, June 25, 1989; in *FBIS*, June 26, 1989).

ZHANG Xingming, an engineer at a farm machinery plant in Guiyang City, was arrested cn June 24, reportedly for sending anonymous "counter-revolutionary" letters to government officials and party leaders since July 1987. In the letters, Zhang allegedly attacked party and government officials. He has been charged with inciting "counter-revolutionary propaganda" and "insulting individuals" (*Agence France Presse*, June 25, 1989; in *FBIS*, June 26, 1989).

On June 23, the Yangpu District People's Court sentenced six defendants to prison terms for "inciting the masses," "sabotaging vehicles," "gathering together a bunch of hoodlums to make trouble," and "obstructing public order" during the first ten days of June. **LIU Yajie**, a young worker at a plant under the

Shanghai Harbor Bureau, reportedly shouted "reactionary slogans" and let the air out of the tires of a trolley bus. He was charged with "gathering together hoodlums to disrupt traffic order" and sentenced to five years in prison, with deprivation of political rights for one year. Three other defendants, YU Jiasong, GU Peijun and ZHANG Kebin were sentenced to three to four years in prison (Shanghai City Service, June 23, 1989; in *FBIS*, June 26, 1989).

The Beijing People's Broadcasting Station reported that five persons, including ZHANG Yansheng and BAI Fengying, were arrested on June 21. The five are accused of attacking official reporters stationed at the Headquarters of the Armed Police Forces who were videotaping the events of June 4. The five reportedly beat the reporters and destroyed their equipment (Beijing Domestic Service, June 22, 1989; in *FBIS*, June 23, 1989).

WANG Xinlin, 24, a former officer of the People's Liberation Army, was reported to have been arrested by the Jinggangshan City Public Security Bureau on the charge of carrying out "anti-revolutionary propaganda activities." Wang was born in Jinggangshan and was a graduate of the PLA Engineering Institute in Chansha in 1987, and a platoon leader until his dismissal from that position last November. He is accused of having put up "reactionary" posters on June 5 at the former residence of Chairman Mao in Jingganshan, and on wire poles along highways and in the lobbies of long-distance coaches. He has also been accused of "viciously attacking" party and state leaders and shouting "reactionary" slogans. The case is reportedly being "further investigated and handled" (Nanchang Jiangxi Provincial Service, June 22, 1989; in *FBIS*, June 23, 1989).

YANG Dongju, a worker at the overhaul unit of the engineering section of the Shenyang Railway Bureau, and QUAN Baogui, a worker at the No. 4 vehicle parts plant of Dandong City, were arrested recently by the Dandong City public security organ reportedly for giving "inciting speeches and spreading rumors in the streets." During the previous week, the Dandong television station reportedly broadcast a videotape of Yang and Quan giving "incitement speeches on the street." After an initial investigation, Yang was reportedly punished by receiving a warning and a "demerit" for alleged participation in gambling and damaging public property. Quan was reportedly punished by receiving a "demerit in line with administrative action" and dismissed from the party (Shenyang Liaoning Provincial Service, June 22, 1989; in *FBIS*, June 23, 1989).

According to Amnesty International, WANG Di, 42, was arrested on June 11 at Dalian, a city in the province of Liaoning. He had spoken with a foreign television crew in Beijing about the June 4 massacre of civilians by the army. Excerpts of the interview were broadcast on Chinese Television on June 10. On June 11, Chinese Television broadcast his arrest and described him as a "dangerous counter-revolutionary instigator."

ZHANG Renfu, a worker at the Shanghai aquatic products cold storage plant; **ZHENG Liang;** and six other members of the "illegal" Shanghai Patriotic Worker Support Group, organized on May 24, 1989 were sentenced to two to eight years in prison. The date of sentencing is unknown; all are believed to have been arrested in mid-June 1989. Zhang and Zheng were found guilty of organizing illegal demonstrations, spreading political rumors and setting up roadblocks, thus disrupting traffic and social order. Another key member, **GONG Xiancheng** (Chencheng) was exempted from punishment because he had turned himself in (*FBIS*, November 22, 1989). In all, sixty-six members of illegal organizations in Shanghai were reportedly detained; 26 of them were arrested formally.

NIU Shengchang, 38, a villager from the Niulin Village in Yunshang Township in Dongping County was arrested on June 16. He is accused of having gone to Beijing on 18 May to join the Peasants Autonomous Union. He returned to his home on June 4, but then reportedly traveled to other localities where he posted "reactionary" posters and distributed "counter-revolutionary leaflets" (Jinan Shandong Provincial Service, June 17, 1989; in *FBIS*, June 20, 1989).

PENG Jing, member of the Beijing "Dare-to-Die Corps" was arrested in Wuhan on June 16. A worker at the Wuhan City Pharmaceutical Factory, he was detained and fined by public security organs on several occasions for committing theft. The Beijing television service which reported his arrest on June 18 showed Peng being brought into a room where he was questioned by two uniformed men (Beijing Television Service, June 18, 1989; in *FBIS*, June 20, 1989).

ZHANG Guorong, leader of Anhui's Hefei City Workers Spontaneous Group, reportedly turned himself in to the Public Security Bureau on June 10. Described as a young worker, he had been detained twice before, and had once been sent to the "education through labor center." He has been accused of "taking advantage of the social unrest" to stage demonstrations, shout slogans, incite strikes and vilify party and state leaders (Beijing Domestic Service, June 13, 1989; in *FBIS*, June 22, 1989).

HAO Fuyuan, 37, a peasant from the Haojia village of Tianzhen Town in

Gaoqing County, was reportedly detained recently for interrogation by the Public Security Bureau for "spreading reactionary statements and inciting peasants to create disturbances." It is not known whether he remains in detention (Jinan Shandong Provincial Service, June 19, 1989; in *FBIS*, June 21, 1989).

XU Bingli, 51, a worker at the Hongkou District Housing Management Company in Shanghai, was arrested in Shanghai on June 13, according to Amnesty International. He is accused of setting up an illegal organization, the China Civil Rights Autonomous Federation, and of making "counter-revolutionary" speeches.

LIU Zihou, 33, a staff member of the Beijing Aquatic Products Company, was arrested on June 18 together with 15 others, "mostly vagrants and idlers," and accused of being the head of the "Capital Workers Special Picket Corps," according to a report from *Xinhua News Agency* (*FBIS*, June 19, 1989). The corps was said to be an offshoot of an organization called the "Beijing Citizens Hunger Strike Corps" which set up tents at Tiananmen Square. The group was accused of setting up roadblocks to stop the army from enforcing martial law and helping erect the "Goddess of Democracy" statue. They tried to flee Beijing after troops moved into the Square on June 3-4, according to a radio broadcast in Beijing.

ZHOU Endong, alias **ZHOU Bo**, aged 20, was arrested on June 9 by the Public Security Bureau in Yinchuan City, Ningxia Hui Nationality Autonomous Region. He was a worker in a Tianjin cable factory. Zhou arrived in Yinchuan from Beijing on June 7, according to the report, and made speeches in front of the Statue of Heroes and Heroines there, claiming to have been an eyewitness to the massacre. The report said he had admitted upon interrogation that he had not been at the Square and had spread rumors that 20,000 had died to incite workers and students to create rebellion.

ZHU Yunfeng, a worker at the Service Committee of Fushun Carbon Plant, was arrested in Fushun City, Liaoning on June 15, together with five other members of an organization called the "People's Corps." They were accused of blocking traffic and shouting slogans such as "Down with official speculation!"

TIAN Suxin, a worker in a plant of the Fushun Steel Plant and two others were also arrested in Fushun City (date not known) for having shouted slogans and blocked traffice on May 17-18 in Fushun City. According to Liaoning radio on June 15, Tian and the two others "brutally beat" those who refused to shout the slogans they provided. All were sentenced to 2 to 3 years of re-education through labor.

ZHANG Jun, a self-employed worker, was arrested on June 14 in Chuxiong, according to the same report. Under the name of Tang Shije, he wrote for *Qinghai Wenxue Bao* and was editor in chief of *Xiaoxi Bao* and *Xinfeng Zaobao*, newspapers which apparently circulated during demonstrations in Kunming.

Five workers were arrested in Jinan City on June 15: **LIU Yubin, CHE Honglian, ZHANG Xinchao, SHAO Liangchen** and **HAO Jingguang.** All had been involved with the Workers Self-Governing Federation of Jinan City and the Workers Democratic Federation. A Jinan radio report (*FBIS*, June 16, 1989) said an amalgam of the two organizations planned to seize political power by armed force. **LIU Yubin** was a worker at the Qianqiaoju Textile Company of Jinan. He and Che Honglian were named as the leaders of the group.

LI Mingxian was arrested on June 16 in Fushun City, Liaoning. A 30-year-old jobless worker from Gaixian County, he entered Beijing on May 13 and joined the "counter-revolutionary rebellion" there on June 3-4. He was captured in Beijing but escaped and fled to Fushun via Yingkou (*FBIS*, June 16, 1989).

ZHAO Guoliang and **HAN Yanjun** were arrested by the Public Security Bureau in Chifeng City on June 5. Zhao, 22, was a self-employed garment seller from Wuhai City, according to a Hohot, Inner Mongolia radio broadcast, and had participated in the "Dare-to-Die Corps" in Tiananmen Square. The broadcast said he kidnapped two public security personnel and stormed the Beijing Public Security Bureau. He was also accused of helping student leader Chai Ling leave Tiananmen Square on June 4. Han Yanjun, 24, from Dingzhou City, Hebei also had been a member of the Dare-to-Die Corps. He was accused of spreading rumors that martial law troops had "caused bloodshed" in Tiananmen Square. He and Zhou left for Chifeng by train on June 4, according to the report (*FBIS*, June 19, 1989).

HE Qunyin and **YOU Dianqi,** two "core members" of the Beijing independent workers' association were captured in Xi'an on June 14, according to a UPI report. Both were accused of taking part in a May 28 protest outside Beijing police headquarters to demand the release of detained workers. They were also accused of attacking army troops.

On June 13, a leader of the Beijing Workers Autonomous Federation named **LIU Huanwen,** 28, was arrested in Shijiazhuang after fleeing Beijing on June 9, according to the *Hong Kong Standard* (June 17, 1989). In his possession were reportedly passes signed by Wuer Kaixi, one of the 21 "most wanted" students. Liu Huanwen had been a worker at the Special Steel Branch Company of the Capital Iron and Steel Company but had received unemployment insurance since the end of 1987 according to a June 14 broadcast of Beijing television (*FBIS*, June 15, 1989). He was accused of having incited sit-ins and demonstrations. He was arrested at 10 PM by police of the Yongan Street Police Station of the Qiaoxi Sub-bureau of the Shijiazhuang City Public Security Bureau after citizens reported his presence.

LIU Congshu, a leader of the Xi'an Workers' Self-Government Federation was arrested around June 11, according to a Xi'an radio broadcast (June 12, 1989) and accused of inciting citizens to "besiege" the Xi'an City Federation of Trade Unions, smash its signboard and go on strike. According to the radio, "the reactionary declaration made by this group of people and their letter to all workers throughout the city viciously attacked the leaders of the party and state in an organized, planned and guided way."

On June 10, **ZHU Huiming**, **LI Huling** and **RUI Tonghu** were arrested together with seven others in Nanjing, according to a June 10 broadcast of Xinhua News Agency. All were members of the Autonomous Workers Federation which had established contacts with the Nanjing Autonomous College Students Federation, according to the report. The radio broadcast singled out the three of the 10 arrested who had previous convictions: Zhu was a vagrant who had been detained for "beating other people"; he was accused of fabricating a story that his brother had been killed in Beijing. Li was a worker in the No.1 farm under the Nanjing City Public Transportation Company who had served two years of "education through labor" for fighting. Rui, a leader of the workers pickets, was a self-employed car repairman who had served one year in prison in 1979 for "injuring people," according to the report.

LI Rongfu, also from Shanghai, was arrested on June 7 and accused of instigating students to sabotage various means of transportation, according to Shanghai Radio. The 39-year-old taxi driver approached a group of students gathered at the intersection of Siping and Xingang Roads, according to the radio and urged them to adopt new "struggle tactics" including setting up roadblocks.

SONG Ruiyang, a woman inspector from Jonghu Steel Mill, was arrested on June 7, according to Shanghai Radio (June 10, 1989). She is accused of having "spread rumors and instigated onlookers" during a demonstration, stopped cars and deflated their tires, and "falsely claimed that her son was killed in Beijing."

143

LIU Jian*, a worker of the No.1 Shanghai Aluminum Alloy Plant, ZHU Genhao, of the Shanghai Shipping Corporation, and CHENG Qiyang, occupation unknown, were arrested between June 6 and June 9, accused of setting up road blocks in Shanghai and instigating others to do the same. Cheng alone was accused of letting the air out of the tires of 36 vehicles apparently during a demonstration to protest the Beijing massacre.

XIAO Bin, 42, an unemployed factory worker, was sentenced on July 13 to 10 years' imprisonment and three years' deprivation of political rights by the Dalian City Middle-level People's Court. He was convicted of "propagating counterrevolutionary lies," according to a UPI report, after reportedly saying that 20,000 people had been killed on June 4. He had been arrested on June 10 in Dalian after having been interviewed by ABC News on the Tiananmen Square massacre. The ABC broadcast showed him imitating how machine guns had mowed down demonstrators. He was turned in shortly after Beijing television appealed to viewers to turn him in for rumor-mongering. A report in the English-language China Daily, a government paper, called him a salesman with Dalian Xinghai Aluminum Window Factory.

An article in People's Daily (August 10, 1989) defended the 10-year sentence against Xiao. It said Xiao had been found guilty of the crime of counter-revolutionary incitement which he had engaged in out of resentment and personal frustration at having been dismissed from his job. The article then quoted from his "confession" which was almost certainly forced. He said he discussed with students in Tiananmen Square how corrupt the government was and said the officers and soldiers responsible for martial law must be killed. Xiao "confessed" he had said this in order "to make the masses doubt the Communist Party and the government," and he told the court he had spread untrue rumors. Under Article 102 of the Criminal Code, such action had to be punished by five to 15 years' imprisonment, and so the sentence Xiao received of ten years was, according to the article, "reasonable, justifiable and lawful, as well as appropriate."

In another arrest in Shanghai, a worker named SHEN Zhigao, an employee of the Shanghai Toy Company warehouse, was arrested on June 11 for spreading counter-revolutionary propaganda at the People's Square and the Finance and Economics University. He was also accused of carrying out unspecified "instigation" at the gate of Tongji University in Shanghai.

WANG Wei and ZHANG Jun*, two members of a "Citizen's Dare-to-Die

Corps" in Beijing were arrested on June 11 by the Martial Law Enforcement Command acting in coordination with the Public Security Bureau, according to a Beijing television broadcast on June 12. Zhang is a native of Hebei and had been in Tiananmen Square every night from May 20 until the army assault on June 3-4. He was accused of "shielding" the radio station there and spreading rumors against the party and government. Wang was reported to be a leader of the "No.9 Team" of the "Dare-to-Die Corps" and was accused of assaulting soldiers with bottles on the night of June 3. "On June 5, while leading corps members in escorting ringleaders of the Autonomous Union of College Students in Beijing to flee to other places, he unscrupulously spread "counter-revolutionary" rumors about a bloodbath on Tiananmen Square aboard the train," the broadcast reported (*FBIS*, June 14, 1989).

YANG Fuqian, 27, a leader of the independent workers association in Beijing, was also arrested on June 10. A worker at the Beijing No. 4 Hydraulic Plant, Yang became a member of the association on May 22, according to Beijing Radio, and was appointed leader of the third picket detachment. The radio report said Yang made a "preliminary confession" that he had instigated people to storm the Beijing Public Security Bureau (police headquarters). That "confession" may have been extracted by force or intimidation. Yang appeared on a state television program in the presence of an interrogator on June 11, and according to a *UPI* report, "The prisoner was groggy and his speech was slurred from an apparent beating that swelled his right cheek. Several of the other suspects also appeared to have suffered beatings."

GAO Yunming, 31, was among 37 persons arrested in Shenyang on June 8, according to a Xinhua radio report broadcast on June 9. He was a worker in the Mutual Inductance Instrument Factory in Shenyang City and was one of eight out of the 37 who will be tried; the others will be released after re-education, according to the report.

HUANG Jianhu, an assembly worker at the water meter plant of the Shanghai Water Company, was arrested on June 8 for directing a "flying vehicle squad" to set up road barricades, according to Shanghai Radio (June 10, 1989). Squad members, some 200 in all, shouted "reactionary slogans" and incited workers to strike, according to the radio.

LI Weiguo, 22, a peasant from Shili village, Mazhai township, Juancheng county, Shandong, was arrested on June 8 for having taken part in the Beijing "Dare-to-Die Corps" and for distributing leaflets about "The Truth of June 3" in front of the Heze Specialized Teachers School. According to Shandong radio, Li went to Beijing on May 15 to support the student hunger strikers. He made contact there with students from Heze and through them entered the "Dare-to-die Corps," the radio said. On June 5, he left Beijing to go to Qingdao and Yantai to make contact with unidentified persons. He returned to Heze on June 8 and was promptly arrested, according to the report.

On June 9, nine worker leaders in Shanghai were arrested. The nine, including **CHEN Shengfu, WANG Miaogen** and **WANG Hong***, were leaders of the Shanghai Self-governing Council of Trade Unions, according to a Beijing Radio broadcast (*FBIS*, June 12, 1989). They are accused of holding secret meetings, advocating strikes, and chanting reactionary slogans. According to the radio, "They also vilified the Shanghai Council of Trade Unions as being totally paralyzed."

CHEN Jinliang, LI Yi, MA Zhiqiang, SUN Xisheng, WANG Baomei, YANG Jian and **ZHANG Hongfu**, all members of the Shanghai Workers Autonomous Federation (probably the same body as that mentioned in the preceding paragraph), are alleged to have held secret meetings, advocated strikes and chanted reactionary slogans (*Renmin Ribao* June 11, 1989; *Jiefang Ribao* August 25, 1989; Amnesty International Urgent Action: 181). DAI Zhenping, accused of "spreading rumors" in connection with the deaths of demonstrators on June 6, 1989 at the Shanghai railway station, has also been arrested (*Jiefang Ribao*, August 23, 1989). The date of his arrest is uncertain, but he, too, may have been seized on June 9 along with Wang Miaogen and the other Shanghai worker leaders. According to the reports, Wang and Dai, along with Chen Shengfu and Cai Chaojun were instrumental in organizing the Workers Federation on May 25; Zhang and Sun with nine others planned the strikes and traffic disruptions on June 5; Wang, in a June 8 public meeting, asked people to organize to overthrow the government; Dai gathered 300 people at Zhabei Hospital to recover the bodies of those killed by trains; and Ma, Chen, Li and Yang planned to organize a "People's Party," committed to military struggle. The organization was declared illegal on June 9.

FU Liyong has been identified as another of the workers arrested in Shanghai for blocking traffic and deflating tires on June 6 (*Jiefang Ribao*, August 23, 1989).

CAI Chaojun, named by the Shanghai Municipal Public Security Bureau as the founder of the Shanghai Workers Autonomous Federation is believed to be in custody. The Hong Kong paper *Zhongguo Tongxun* reported on August 16, 1989 that authorities in Shanghai had discovered that Cai, a jobless man who had just been released from a labor camp, was the founder of the Shanghai Workers Voluntary Supporting Group which later became the Shanghai Workers Autonomous Federation.

CHEN Dao, JIANG Zhi'an, DAI Yue and **YANG Xiuping** have been arrested for organizing a broadcasting station, Voice of Democracy and Freedom, in Shanghai's People's Square. The dates and places of their arrests are unknown. Jiang, a worker for the Shanghai Construction Company's 301 Team, and the others are said to have begun "counterrevolutionary propaganda broadcasts" on May 23, 1989 (*Jiefang Ribao*, August 23, 1989).

CHEN Deqing has been arrested for blocking and attacking trains in Shanghai on June 6, 1989. According to a report in *Jiefang Ribao* (August 23), Chen joined with others from Shanghai to show support for pro-democracy demonstrators in Beijing. The date of his arrest is unknown.

FAN Jinchun, another Shanghai worker, has been arrested and accused of spreading such rumors as "Police beat people" and "Deng Xiaoping was killed" (*Jiefang Ribao*, August 23, 1989). No additional details are available.

GAO Guihong, a Shanghai worker, was arrested for inciting people to block trains on June 6, 1989. The incident allegedly occured after six demonstrators in Shanghai had already been killed by trains (*Jiefang Ribao*, August 23, 1989). The date of Gao's arrest is unknown.

LI Jian*, a self-employed Shanghai worker, was sentenced to three-and-a-half years imprisonment for shouting revolutionary slogans, deflating tires and blocking traffic on June 5, 1989 (*Jiefang Ribao*, July 15, 1989). Neither the date of arrest nor of sentencing is known.

TANG Guoliang was sentenced on July 6, 1989 to ten years' imprisonment. According to *Jiefang Ribao* (July 13, 1989), the 29-year-old unemployed Tang, while pretending to be a Shanghai Railroad Institute student on June 6, incited people to block trains.

WU Qihao, a Shanghai worker, and **LÜ Guodong** were arrested for their alleged June 8 attempt to lower the flag on the Huangpu District Government building out of respect for victims of the Beijing massacre (*Jiefang Ribao*, August 23, 1989). Arrest dates are unknown.

YANG Jinfa, a Shanghai resident, has been sentenced to eleven years imprisonment for spreading rumors, making trouble, shouting counterrevolutionary slogans, disturbing the social order and attacking the police (*Jiefang Ribao*, August 23, 1989). Neither the date of the alleged incident nor the dates of arrest or sentencing are known.

YANG Tingfen, a railroad worker in the East Shanghai Work Area has been arrested for helping student demonstrators to block and damage military railroad tracks on June 5, 1989 (*Jiefang Ribao*, August 23, 1989). The date of Yang's arrest is unknown.

YAN Tinggui, one of ten members of the Shanghai Patriotic Workers Organization Supporting Beijing People, has been arrested for allegedly forcing the director of his factory to call a strike in support of the people of Beijing following the crackdown there. According to *Jiefang Ribao* (August 23, 1989), Yan had a previous gambling conviction for which the Shanghai government paper had labeled him a "bad element."

YAO Shanbo, a peasant from Xinghua, Jiangsu Province, has been sentenced to four years' imprisonment for joining the Shanghai riot on June 5, 1989. He is alleged to have blocked traffic, deflated tires, and shouted counterrevolutionary slogans (*Jiefang Ribao*, July 15, 1989).

ZHAO Guozheng has been arrested and accused of blocking traffic and deflating tires on June 8, 1989, in connection with the Shanghai demonstrations in support of Beijing's pro-democracy movement (*Jiefang Ribao*, August 23, 1989). The date of Zhao's arrest is unknown.

BAI Dongping, a 27-year-old Beijing train attendant and a member of the central committee of the Beijing Workers Autonomous Federation, was first arrested on May 28, 1989 but released after 3000 people demonstrated outside the Public Security Bureau. He is reported to have been re-arrested in Zhongjiang County, Sichuan Province while on the run. The date of his second arrest is unknown. (Reference in the press to "Bai Leping" is probably in error and refers to Bai Dongping.)

On June 8, four members of the Shanghai-based "Patriotic Volunteer Army" were arrested. They had taken part in a demonstration on the Bund the evening of June 8, claiming that 200,000 troops were on their way to suppress the students, according to a Shanghai Radio report. One of them, a private entrepreneur named **ZHANG Qiwang,** was a member of the Autonomous Union of Workers. He was released from an earlier jail term in January 1988. According the the radio report, he had incited people to take the bodies of victims killed in a June 6 riot from hospital mortuaries.

Also on June 8, Beijing television reported that eight members of a youth "Dare-to-Die Corps" were arrested in Taipei, Harbin, Heilongjang Province. They had ridden through the streets reportedly shouting, "Long Live Dao Qiang Pao"; Dao Qiang Pao translates as "Knife, Gun, Artillery" and according to television was the name of a gang responsible for murder and arson.

HU Liangbin was arrested in Wuhan, Hubei on June 7 together with several others for overturning trucks, blocking traffic and setting fire to a public vehicle. Hu is unemployed. Arrested with him were YANG Gechuang, CHEN Wei, and JIN Tao.

One worker is reported to have been arrested in Shanghai on May 31 for making a pro-democracy speech; his name is SHEN Jizhong, a florist in his 40's. No other details about him are available, and it is not known whether he was released before the June 3-4 crackdown.

Other workers arrested include GAO Jintang, ZHU Guanghua, and LI Xiaohu, from the Hangzhou Autonomous Workers' Association.

Three people have been arrested for killing a soldier in Beijing: ZHAO Yuetang, a peasant; YANG Zhizen, a worker; and LI Weidong, unemployed.

Amnesty International has reported the following arrests of workers:

HE Heng and HU Jiahao were arrested in Shanghai on June 7-8, allegedly for obstructing vehicles with roadblocks, deflating the tires of five vehicles and beating up the drivers.

HU Kesheng was arrested on June 7-8 in Shanghai allegedly for forcibly stopping a truck, and attempting to use it as a roadblock. DONG Jin was also arrested in Shanghai on June 7-8, allegedly for having deflated the tires of a vehicle in order to block a road.

HU Linyong, KONG Qiming, Xu Guibao, SHEN Minggui, and LIU Ronglin were arrested in Shanghai on June 5-6, allegedly for causing destruction to vehicles.

LU Zhongshu and HUANG Lianxi were arrested in Beijing on June 6. The charges against them are, respectively, burning army trucks and armoured vehicles, and setting fire to the seats of a trolley bus.

GAN Huijie was arrested in Beijing on June 3, allegedly for attacking members of the armed forces.

SUN Yancai, GONG Chuanchang, and LIAN Zhenguo were arrested in Beijing on June 10, allegedly for looting.

KANG Yaoqing was arrested in Beijing (date unknown), allegedly for smashing and burning military vehicles.

XIAO Zhongwu and QU Yutang were arrested in Harbin, in Heilongjiang Province, on June 10 allegedly for inciting passengers to destroy a bus.

6. ARRESTS OF ALLEGED TAIWAN AGENTS

LIANG Chaotian was arrested as an alleged secret KMT agent in November 1989 in Yunnan Province. He has reportedly confessed to his crimes and is awaiting trial. According to *Xinhua* (January 13, 1990 in FBIS January 16, 1990), Liang, a native of Longchun County, Yunnan collaborated with the US-based "Chinese Alliance for Democracy" in carrying out sabotage. He is said to have joined the Mainland Task Force of the KMT in 1981, and at the end of 1986, together with **WANG Bingzhang** and **KE Lisi,** already active in the Alliance, formed its Northern Burma Branch. Liang, as director, reportedly sent people into Yunnan to conduct espionage activities; during the pro-democracy uprising he distributed "reactionary propaganda materials" in a plot to enlarge the disturbances. There is no additional information about either Wang or Ke.

YANG Xiaohua, 30, was arrested in Yichang City, Hubei on charges of being a spy for Taiwan, according to a Wuhan, Hubei radio broadcast. Yang, who until 1985 was a member of the Yichang City song and dance company, was allegedly recruited by Taiwan's intelligence service while he was on one of several trips abroad. During the student demonstrations of May and June, according to the report, Yang mixed with students from Yichang city and "instigated them to storm local party and government organs." He also wrote propaganda materials, according to the report. Evidence of his espionage activities was found when his home was searched, the radio said.

OU Zongyou, a Taiwanese businessman, was arrested on June 22 in Guiyang, according to *Xinhua News Agency.* He was accused of spying for Taiwan, spreading rumors, slandering the Chinese Communist Party, collecting banned publications and taking pictures of "anti-state demonstrations." According to *UPI, Xinhua* said Ou was a member of Taiwan's Military Intelligence Bureau and had received espionage training in Hong Kong.

LIANG Qiang, (previously mispelled Qiyang), **WANG Changhong** and **QIAN Rongmian** accused of being Taiwan agents, were given heavy sentences on January 4, 1990 (*Xinhua,* January 4 in *Shijie Ribao,* January 4) by the Beijing Intermediate Court (Beijing Television Service, January 4, in FBIS January 5). Liang, 36, a Beijing factory cadre, sentenced to 15 years and three years deprivation of political rights, is said to have joined the KMT's Mainland Work spy unit in October 1986 and returned to Beijing in November of that year.

During April and May, 1989 he allegedly collected intelligence in Beijing and wrote reactionary articles for the Beijing Students Autonomous Federation and the Autonomous Workers Federation with the aim of inciting students and others to rebel. At the time of his arrest, May 27, 1989, he was allegedly preparing a manifesto for a new "Chinese Solidarity" Party. Wang, a 38-year-old Beijing factory cadre, also received a 15 year sentence and three years deprivation of political rights. He is alleged to have joined the spy network in January 1989, arriving in Beijing on assignment on April 17. During the uprising, Wang reportedly recruited Qian as a spy. Qian, also a Beijing factory cadre, received a six year sentence and was deprived of his political rights for one year. He was arrested in Zhangjiakou.

ZHANG Yi and WU Jidong, Guangzhou residents and alleged Taiwan agents, were sentenced for spying on October 23, 1989 by the Guangzhou Municipal Intermediate People's Court. Wu, 23, an employee of a Guangzhou guesthouse, received a ten year sentence and three years deprivation of political rights. Zhang, an unemployed 25-year-old, received thirteen years and four years' deprivation of rights. Both men allegedly joined a KMT special agent organization in October 1988. During May and June 1989, they allegedly used a secret code to report to the KMT Taiwan organization on the Beijing and Guangzhou student movements (Guangzhou Guangdong Provincial Service, February 3, 1990, in FBIS, February 5).

Xinhua reports the sentencing in Shanghai on February 21, 1990 of five men accused of spying for Taiwan. ZHOU Yan (mistakenly reported as Zhan Yan), identified as the group's leader, received a life sentence; CAI Weiguo was sentenced to a five year term; three others, presumably QIU Lin (or Qiu Liu), LU Zhengqing, and FENG Jun (or Feng Jin) all charged with espionage in the same case (Shanghai City Service, January 13, 1990 in FBIS January 16), received sentences ranging from ten to 15 years. Zhou, 23, a worker, allegedly joined the secret service in March 1988 and was provided funds for espionage activities. He is reported to have recruited Cai and others in September 1988, and Lu and Feng in February 1989; and to have passed on information about the Shanghai riots, allegedly collected by Lu, Feng and others. Qiu, 30, described as a former Shanghai reporter (*Renmin Ribao, Overseas Edition*, June 23, 1989) allegedly became a secret agent in June 1988 and stole into China the following September. He was assigned to collect intelligence and recruit new agents for which purposes he was provided funds for cameras, video-cassette recorders and secret writing instruments. He is said to have actively collected intelligence during the "turmoil" (the official term for the pro-democracy movement), in Shanghai in spring and summer 1989.

QIAO Xiaoshi and QU Zuojie, two alleged Taiwan agents, were reportedly arrested on June 22, 1989. The disposition of their cases is unknown.

7. ARRESTS OF CATHOLICS AND PROTESTANTS

Arrests and disappearances of Catholic Church personnel unaffiliated with the official China Catholic Patriotic Association and loyal to the Vatican have been reported by the *Hong Kong Standard* (January 9, 1990) and *Shijie Ribao* (January 10 and January 16). Two arrests were confirmed on January 9, 1990 by top officials of the organization. **Father Anthony ZHANG Guangyi,** 83, a parish priest from Sanyuan County, Shaanxi Province was arrested for "political reasons" at 2 a.m. on December 11, 1989. Zhang allegedly said "something wrong" at a religious meeting. **Bishop Joseph LI Xide,** (also given as **Li Side**) head of the Catholic Church in Tianjin since November 1989, was arrested at home in Tianjin during the night of December 8-9. Called to administer last rites, Li was seized by a large contingent of public security personnel as he left his home (Amnesty International UA 514/89, December 28, 1989). His present whereabouts are unknown. The China Catholic Patriotic Association has stressed that Li's arrest was for "religious reasons."

According to the Hong Kong-based Union of Catholic Asian News, six additional clergymen and church leaders from northern China have also been arrested; another has disappeared. **Bishop Peter LIU Guangdong,** appointed Bishop of Yixian district, Hebei Province in 1982, was arrested on November 26, 1989 in Baoding, Hebei. He has not been heard from since. Bishop **JIA Zhiguo,** a native of Luan Xian, Hebei Province was arrested in Beijing on April 7. **Father SHI Wende** (also given as **Shi Wande**), **Father SU Jimin** (also given as **Su Zemin**) and lay leader **WANG Dongshan,** (also given as **Wang Tongshan**) all of Hebei Province were arrested in Beijing in December, 1989. Su had recently been appointed vicar-general of the Baoding diocese. **Father PEI Rongqui** (also given as **Pei Kongqui**), 50, on the wanted list since April 1989, was in hiding for more than four months before being arrested in Beijing on September 3. Pei, a Trappist parish priest who lived and worked in Yutong Village near Baoding, Hebei Province, refused to join the official China Catholic Patriotic Association. He had previously had a confrontation with police who came to destroy his church (a tent) on April 18. During the raid, over 300 people were reportedly injured, two died, and about 30 were arrested (Amnesty International UA 514/89, December 28, 1989). **Bishop Peter Joseph FAN Xueyan,** 82, from Baoding, disappeared on December 11 after being taken away by local police authorities. Fan, appointed bishop of Baoding in 1951 was arrested for the first time in 1957. He was released on parole in 1987; his whereabouts during the intervening 30 years are unclear.

Four additional bishops, loyal to the Vatican, have also been arrested according to *Shijie Ribao* (January 17, 1990). **Bishop JIANG Liren,** from Hohhot, Inner Mongolia, joined the church last year; **Bishop LU Zhengsheng,** from Tianshui, Gansu Province joined in 1983; **Bishop YANG Lipo,** from Lanzhou, Gansu, in 1981; and **Bishop YU Chenggai** (also given as **Yu Chengdi**), from Hanzhong, Hubei Province, in 1961. The dates of their arrests are unknown. A fifth Bishop, **LI Zhenrong,** also of Gansu, was reportedly arrested in December 1989 (FBIS January 22, 1990).

The Union of Catholic Asian News (FBIS, January 22, 1990) has also reported the arrest of **Bishop GUO Wenzhi** in Qiqihar, Heilongjiang Province on December 14, 1989. Guo was reportedly first arrested in Beijing in 1954; released in 1964; and re-arrested in 1966 and sent to a reform-through-labor camp in the Xinjiang Autonomous Region. He was last released in 1979 and returned to Hebei Province where he taught foreign languages until 1985.

Officials of the State Council's Religious Affairs Bureau confirmed on February 7, 1990 that some Catholics had been arrested, but insisted the detentions have nothing to do with religious beliefs. Rather, those arrested were said to have broken the law by obeying papal authority in defiance of China's constitution which forbids "foreign domination" in religious affairs. According to the spokespersons, no details as to names, places of arrest or charges are available (FBIS, February 8, 1990).

Chinese authorities in Guangzhou have closed an underground Protestant church according to a report in *Shijie Ribao* (February 27, 1990). A religious official in Guangzhou said **LIN Qiangao,** a "self-styled "Protestant priest" had been conducting services in his home, but on February 22, the "church," normally attended by about 100 people, was shuttered. Lin has not been arrested, the official continued, but he has been warned to cease his religious activities.

8. ARRESTS OF TIBETAN ACTIVISTS*

LOBSANG TENZIN (Blo-bzang bstan-'dzin), a 22-year-old student at Tibet University at the time of his arrest on April 16, 1988, is reportedly facing imminent execution, according to an Asia Watch source. Sentenced to death on January 19, 1989 for his part as "principal culprit" in the death of a Chinese officer on March 5, 1988 during violent demonstrations in Lhasa, Lobsang Tenzin's was given a two year reprieve reportedly ending on the anniversary date of the alleged crime. **SONAM WANGDO** (Bsod-nams dbang-'dus), a member of the Lhasa Political Consultative Conference, was accused as Lobsang Tenzin's accomplice and arrested at the same time. He received a life sentence. Four other rioters received sentences of 15 years; 13 were sentenced to 14 years' imprisonment; five received three year terms.

GONG La, a female student at Tibet University, was reportedly so severely injured by prison guards while in custody that she has had to be hospitalized, reportedly sometime in September 1989 (*Reuters,* October 22, 1989). The nature of her injuries are, however, uncertain, although unconfirmed reports say she has been crippled. Her family has had to meet all hospital and medical expenses and has had to agree to return her to custody if and when she recovers. Gong was arrested sometime after martial law was imposed in March 1989 and sentenced to three years administrative detention for putting up posters calling for independence. Her arrest was confirmed by university president, Ciwang Junmei; the nature of her sentence means that she was almost certainly sentenced without trial. Gong's present whereabouts are unclear.

Other first-hand accounts of torture and beatings in Tibetan prisons have been well documented by an Asia Watch source.

According to an unattributed article in the *Washington Post* (December 21, 1990), a demonstration by a small group of monks outside the Barkhor Monastery on December 5, 1989 resulted in their arrests.

---

*   There are three different ways of rendering Tibetan names into English. Reports of arrests of Tibetans cite one or more of these, but with little consistency. Here, to facilitate cross-referencing by other concerned groups, we cite all known versions of each name. Thus the following may appear: 1) the general phonetic rendering; 2) the precise transliteration from the written form; and 3) the pinyin version, based on official Chinese press reports. (The latter is the least phonetically accurate and its use is disliked by many Tibetans.) The general phonetic rendering (where available) appears in capitals here. The precise-transliteration and the pinyin version (where available) then follow in parentheses.

Five Tibetan monks, demonstrators for Tibetan independence in Lhasa, have been sent without trial to labor camps for three years. The sentences were announced on November 3, 1989. A sixth monk, **DAWA TSERING** (Zla-ba tshe-ring, Dawaciren), accused of organizing separatist activities, awaits trial (*Tibet Daily*, November 6, as reported by *Reuters*, November 16, 1989; *FBIS*, November 20, 1989). Dawa Tsering and a second monk, **TENZIN** (Bstan-dzin, Danzeng), paraded "illegally" in central Lhasa around Jokhang Temple, Tibet's holiest Buddhist shrine, on September 30 and were arrested on the spot. The latter brandished Tibet's nationalist flag which, he said, his companion had made. Dawa Tsering was also accused of taking part in "rioting" on March 5. The other four, **LICHUO, PURGYAL** (Phur-rgyal, Pujue), **LHAGPA** (Lhag-pa, Laba) and **TRINLEY** ('Phrin-las, Cheli), are accused of shouting "independent Tibet and other reactionary slogans" while parading around the temple on October 25. All six were brought before a mass public meeting in Lhasa on November 3. Tenzin is from Ganden monastery; the others are from Pareburu (Brag-lha klu-phug) monastery.

The arrest of **TSETEN NORGYE** (Tshe-brtan nor-rgyas), a bookkeeper, has been officially confirmed according to an Asia Watch source. Detained sometime in April or May 1989 as a pro-independence leader, Tseten Norgye was formally charged "according to the law" on November 10, 1989. The official announcement accuses Tseten Norgye, originally from Gyantse (Rgyal-r-tse), of joining an "anti-government organization in 1988," the previously unknown Uprising Group for Tibetan Independence, "...and engaging in collecting information for the Dalai Lama Group." It is presumed that he will face charges of espionage, belonging to a "counter-revolutionary" clique and producing "counter-revolutionary" literature on a mimeograph machine at his workplace, the Lhasa Hotel. An informer reportedly told police that Tseten, about 45, who was released in the early 1980's after spending 15 to 20 years in prison, had been distributing Tibetan propaganda. His arrest followed a police search of his home. According to independent sources, Tseten has been held without charge in Chakpori (Lcags-po-ri) prison where he is alleged to have been tortured and to have lost an eye during interrogation.

Three Tibetans, accused of taking part in violent demonstrations in Lhasa on March 5, 1989 were recently sentenced to prison terms (*FBIS*, October 10, 1989). **TENDHAR** (Bstan-dar, Danda), 18, a native of Medro Gongkar (Malgro gong-dkar, Muzhugongke) received six years for stealing religious objects and chanting independence slogans; **DAWA TSERING*** (Zla-ba tshe-ring, Dawachiron), 17, and **DORJE** (Rdo-rje, Duojie), 24, both from Lhasa, received four years each for chanting "reactionary slogans" and for stoning police officials and public buildings.

Eleven Tibetans were sentenced at a mass public meeting in Lhasa on November 30 to terms ranging from five to nineteen years for the "counter-revolutionary" crime of advocating Tibetan independence, according to *Xinhua* (*Reuters*, December 12, 1989). Ten of the eleven are monks from Drepung ('Bras-spungs), Lhasa's largest monastery. The group's leader, NGAWANG BUCHUNG (Ngag-dbang bu-chung, Awang Pingqiong), a Tolungdechen (Stod-lung bde-chen, Doelungdechen) native; and NGAWANG OSEL, (Ngag-dbang 'od-gsal, Awang Weisi) were charged with founding a "counterrevolutionary clique," named Tibetan Independence, in January 1988. Eight others were accused of joining the organization and "collecting intelligence according to foreign demand and printing and distributing reactionary leaflets." They are also said to have "viciously slandered the people's democratic dictatorship." An Asia Watch source reports the leaflets are consistently non-violent in nature and usually confined to reports of Tibetan dissident activity. The two founders, along with five of those sentenced were among the 21 monks who began the current wave of Tibetan unrest on September 27, 1987. All were released in January 1988 after signing confessions admitting to political crimes and acknowledging Chinese sovereignty over Tibet. Ngawang Buchung, 28, received 19 years imprisonment and 9 years deprivation of political rights; Ngawang Osel, 21, 17 years and 5 years deprivation of political rights; **KELSANG DUDU** (Skal-bzang don-grub), 18 years and deprivation of political rights; **JAMPEL CHUNJOR** ('Jam-dpal chos-'byor), 19 years and deprivation of political rights; **NGAWANG GYALTSEN** (Ngag-dbang rgyal-mtshan), 27, 17 years and deprivation of political rights; **JAMPEL LOSEL** ('Jam-dpal blo-gsal), 27, 10 years and 3 years deprivation of political rights; **NGAWANG RINCHEN** (Ngag-dbang rin-chen), 26, 9 years and 3 years deprivation of political rights; **JAMPEL MONLAM** ('Jam-dpal smon-lam), 26, **JAMPEL TSERING** ('Jam-dpal tshe-ring), 22, and **NGAWANG GONGAR** (Ngag-dbang gong-dkar), 5 years and 2 years deprivation of political rights each.

An eleventh man, **DHUNDUP DORJE** (Don-grub rdo-rje, Dunzhu Duoji), a 43-year-old driver at the Lhasa Shoe and Hat Factory, received 5 years and 2 years deprivation of political rights for "counterrevolutionary agitation." He had previously spent 9 months at Gutsa (Dgu-rtsa) prison for his involvement in an independence demonstration on October 1, 1987. It is reported that he was regularly beaten, resulting in partial deafness, and was chained hand and foot for three months in a cell he shared with 20 others.

TASHI TSERING (Bkra-shis tshe-ring), a Shigatse (Gzhis-ka-rtse) native, was arrested November 28, 1989 and is awaiting trial for the "crime of counter-revolutionary propaganda and inflamatory delusion" (Lhasa Tibet Regional Service; in *FBIS*, December 1, 1989). A senior public figure, Tashi, 50, has been charged with producing 73 slogans and leaflets which he deposited in complaint boxes at the central airport, the general office of the CPPCC perfectual committee and the head office of the Shigatse city party committee. According to the report, the leaflets called for independence and "venomously slandered the CPC and the socialist system." Tashi is also said to have been "slack in remolding his ideology." He has been removed as a CPPCC perfectual committee member.

Five middle-school students in Lhasa were arrested on December 8, 1989 according to official Tibet radio (*Reuters*, December 9, 1989; in *FBIS*, December 19, 1989). **Mina TSERING** (tshe-ring), **Dalaba TSERING** (tshe-ring), **Zhonglaba TSERING** (tshe-ring), **Xiaobian TSERING** (tshe-ring) and **TASHI WANGDU** (Bkra-shis dbang-'dus, Zhaixi Wangdui) are accused of forming the Tibet Youth Association (Young Lion Group), an illegal "counterrevolutionary" organization, in March 1988. According to the report, "the students gathered a large amount of reactionary material and banners marked with lions of the snowy mountain which they then posted in many streets, temples and in the school"; furthermore, they "vilified the Chinese Communist Party and called for Tibetan independence."

In a related case, **PHURBU** (Phur-'bu, Pubu), another student at the #1 Secondary School, has been sent by the Lhasa City People's Procuratorate to a "relevant department to undergo labor reform." Although he did not formally join the Young Lion Group, Phurbu is alleged to have taken part in its activities.

DAWA DROLMA (Zla-ba sgrol-ma, Dawazouma), a temporary teacher at the Lhasa City Cement Plant, has been given a suspended sentence by the same court. Dawa allegedly wrote a reactionary song on her classroom blackboard and then taught it to her students. She is also alleged to have provided shelter for rioters. Although her crimes constituted "counterrevolutionary instigation," Dawa has responsibility for feeding a year old son; hence her case will undergo further investigation.

LOYE (Blo-ye, Luoya), a monk at Potala Palace, was sentenced on December 6, 1989 by the Lhasa Intermediate People's Court to 15 years imprisonment and deprivation of political rights for 5 years. He had been charged with "counterrevolutionary propaganda, inflammatory delusion and espionage." According to Lhasa Tibet Regional Service (December 7, 1989; in *FBIS*, December 20, 1989), the 39-year-old Luoya, "actively colllected intelligence for the enemy abroad, instigated the masses to hinder the enforcement of state laws and regulations, and jeopardized national unity."

Six Tibetan nuns and two Tibetan men have been sentenced without trial to terms of up to three years in "labor re-education camps," and two other nuns are still awaiting sentence, according to the *Tibet Daily* of October 18 (*FBIS*, November 1, 1989). Four Buddhist nuns — identified as **Pingzuozongjie, Geshangwangmu, Dangzengjujie** and **Dangzenwangmu** (spellings based on the Chinese language are only approximate) — were charged with having staged an illegal demonstration in central Lhasa on October 14 calling for Tibetan independence; they were each given three year sentences by an extra-judicial organ in Lhasa called the Committee for Re-education through Labor. Two nuns from the Miqiong Monastery arrested during the demonstration, **Pingzuonizheng** and **Pingzuobaimu**, both said to be "ringleaders," are still awaiting sentence. Two men, **Geshangzuoga** and **Cijie**, who allegedly shouted "reactionary" slogans in Lhasa on October 14, were sentenced to 3 and 2 years in re-education camps respectively. In addition, 2 nuns named **Luoshangzuoma** and **Awangjuzheng** were each sentenced to 3 years in re-education camps for staging a demonstration in central Lhasa on October 15 and chanting "reactionary" slogans.

A group of 6 Tibetans were recently tried and sentenced in Lhasa in connection with their pro-independence activities in March of this year, according to *People's Daily* (September 13, 1989). A 22-year-old man was sentenced to life imprisonment for "beating, smashing, looting and burning" during the March unrest, and another was jailed for 12 years for inciting people to sing pro-independence songs. At the trial another 2 Tibetans were sentenced to prison terms of 3 and 4 years for "disseminating counter-revolutionary propaganda."

DANZIN PUNCOG, 33, and OUZHU GYAINCAIN, 37, arrested recently, apparently in Lhasa, Tibet and accused of being secret agents of the Dalai Lama, were also thought to have been sentenced to terms of 5 and 11 years respectively.

A report of their arrests had reached Beijing on August 29, 1989. Danzin Puncog was accused of having been ordered to incite riots during the demonstrations in Lhasa last December on Human Rights Day. He was said to have urged crowds to attack the police station, to have distributed reactionary pamphlets and to have helped injured demonstrators, according to a *Reuters* report (August 29, 1989). Ouzhu is said to have sent intelligence on behalf of the Dalai Lama. Both were said to have "confessed" to working for the Dalai Lama's Ministry of Security.

Seven Tibetans were tried and sentenced for their involvement in demonstrations in Lhasa, Tibet on March 5, 1989. **CERING NGOIZHU**, 57, was accused of spying for the Dalai Lama and sentenced to 12 years in prison on charges of "counter-revolutionary propaganda and inflammatory delusion." During the March demonstration he was said to have incited young people to sing reactionary Tibetan independence songs. **DAGWA**, a lama at Raodoi Monastery in Quxu County, was sentenced on the same charge to four years' imprisonment. He was accused of hanging the Tibetan flag in the monastery and shouting reactionary slogans. **NAMGA**, a lama at the same monastery, was sentenced to three years on the same charges. **DINGLING, DAGWA*** and **GAISANG** were sentenced on September 13 by the Chengguan District Court to five, eight, and four years in prison respectively on charges of "looting and destruction of property" in connection with the March 5 demonstration. **PAS-SANG** was given a life sentence by the Lhasa Intermediate Court for "beating, smashing, looting and burning." His occupation is not known.

In addition, a Tibetan named **NGAWANG GYAINSING**, a lama at the Zhebung Monastery, was sentenced to 5 years for providing information to an alleged intelligence agent for the Dalai Lama, **DANZIN PUNCOG** (see index). The sentence was announced on September 13 by Radio Lhasa.

Two members of the Tibet branch of the Buddhist Association of China were expelled from membership in September after having been tried and sentenced earlier this year. **CHUNG BDAG**, 27, of Dagze County, was sentenced by the Intermediate People's Court of Lhasa to seven years for instigating lamas at the Gnain Monastery to riot in December 1987. **GYULO ZLABATSHERING**, 60, was sentenced last January to ten years in prison for "colluding with reactionaries abroad to try to overthrow the people's government and the socialist system." According to an article in Xinhua News Service (September 21, 1989), Gyulo was sentenced to life imprisonment in 1959 but released under an amnesty twenty years later, in 1979.

A Chinese police official in October 1989 admitted that over 400 Tibetans had been arrested following the pro-independence demonstrations in Lhasa in March 1989. In an interview in Lhasa with Reuters correspondent Guy Dinmore (*Reuters*, October 22, 1989), the police official stated that 63 of the detained Tibetans had already been tried and sentenced, and that about 20 nuns had been sent for "re-education through labor," a form of detention without trial, for periods of up to three years. The official added that 320 of those originally arrested had been released. Previously, Chinese authorities had admitted to having sentenced only 20 men and 11 nuns in Tibet since March. The newly released official figures thus indicate that more than 50 Tibetans have been sentenced since the March unrest without any public notification having been made. Unofficial sources, moreover, estimate the true number of arrests since March in Lhasa alone as well over 1,000. Mr. Dinmore said that he had conducted secret interviews with three Tibetans who had been released from prison in Lhasa; the 3 stated that prison guards there regularly beat inmates and sometimes used torture. Two of his sources bore major scars which they said had been inflicted in prison.

9. OTHERS

LIANG Xiang, governor of Hainan Province and vice-secretary of the Chinese Communist Party in Hainan, has been arrested and forced to write a self-criticism (*Shijie Ribao*, March 1, 1990). He is the highest local official arrested since the June 4 crackdown. According to the report, Liang was arrested on alleged corruption charges. He is said to have given his wife the privilege of buying and selling property; thus using his power to serve his own family. It is believed, however, that Liang's arrest stems from his close connection to Zhao Ziyang. It is speculated that authorities want Liang to provide information about Zhao's activities. Liang is reportedly detained at headquarters of the People's Armed Police.

Shanghai police have arrested two Brazilian-Chinese, **CHI Jusu,** 31, and her brother **JI Youyi,** 30, on suspicion of smuggling citizens out of the country. The two were detained at Hongqiao airport (date unknown) when a group of 43 Chinese they were leading were found to have false visas. Tools and other equipment were recovered from their living quarters in Shanghai. The two, now Brazilian citizens, are said to have "confessed to their illegal activities" (*Xinhua* in *FBIS*, November 8, 1989).

XU Qinxian, head of the Beijing-based 38th Group Army, was reportedly court-martialled and given a "stiff sentence" last autumn for failing to enforce martial law (*South China Morning Post,* December 28, 1989; in *FBIS*, same day). Xu, reportedly the son of the late vice-minister of defense, Xu Guangda, is said to have checked into a hospital soon after the the declaration of martial law on May 20, 1989, protesting he could not carry out orders to supress demonstrators. (FBIS, January 18, 1990). Another 110 officers and 1400 enlisted men also allegedly refused to take orders or left their posts during the People's Liberation Army crackdown, according to Yang Baibing, Chief Political Commissar (*South China Morning Post*, December 28, 1989).

10. INDEX OF NAMES

170